How I Avoided Dialysis
And You Can Too!

HOW I AVOIDED DIALYSIS
And You Can, Too!

Mercedes Hawkins
Lawrenceville, Ga

Disclaimer

All diseases are curable. This includes Kidney disease. I have gotten people off of dialysis. Anyone can do this and you do not have to be a doctor. I am not a doctor. But is is common sense that you don't have to be a doctor to heal yourself. Before the invention of doctors, you had no choice.

Mercedes Hawkins
Lawrenceville, GA 3004

Email: hiad2@yahoo.com.com
www.lulu.com/spotlight/sabia

(678)683-6002

ISBN 978-1-105-53856-8

Table of Contents

Acknowledgement ix

Introduction...xi

Chapter 1.   They Can't Believe I am Still Standing 1

Chapter 2.   How I Found Out I Had Kidney Disease.................3

Chapter 3.   What Causes It...7

Nutrition blockage, antibiotics *10*

Over-the-counter drugs, "heredity" *11*

Meat, acidosis, stress...*13*

High blood pressure *15*

Heavy metals..*17*

Out of touch with body rhythm *17*

Electromagnetic waves, wrong music *18*

Buying propaganda *19*

Alcohol, cigarettes exposure, wrong sugar *20*

Over-eating..*22*

Denatured flour *23*

Pace of eating, not eliminating during .E.P *29*

Lack of oxygen, eating swine..................................*31*

Pollution *32*

Toiletries, cosmetics, processed foods....................*33*

Vaccinations *39*

Chemicals *40*

Pesticides, politics, cooked foods *42*

Caffeine..*44*

Chapter 4.   Straying From The Mother Diet.............................. 45

Chapter 5.   Conventional Treatment...................................... 51
     Problem with dialysis.. 66

Chapter 6.   Replacing Old Habits With Better Ones 67
     Transitional foods, homemade teas 69
     Natural laxatives.. 73
     Becoming a vegetarian 75
     The protein myth 75
     Letting digestive system rest 77
     Aspirin and anti-inflammation substitutes.............. 78
     Mercury fillings replacement................................ 79

Chapter 7.   Inexpensive Remedies....................................... 83
     Cheap ways to detoxify 84
     Natural diuretics.. 86
     Natural laxatives.. 87
     Variety of vegetables.. 88
     Clay.. 91
     Natural metabolizers & excercise......................... 94
     Bitter herbs... 95
     The starch myth: man-made vs nature.................... 96
     Parasite riddance... 98

Chapter 8.   The Price of Good Health 105
     Real salt heals.. 106
     Purify.. 107
     Mineral absorption 109
     Nutrition dense food.. 110
     The best water... 112
     Circulation 115
     Water retention remedies.................................... 125
     Chelation... 128
     DNA repair.. 130

Nutritional counseling *133*

Alkalinize your body *138*

Treating high blood pressure naturally *142*

The price of reverting *159*

Conclusion 163

Bibliography 167

Recommended Readings 169

Index 171

About the Author 175

Acknowledgements

I am especially thankful to Michael Worthington for telling me about Queen Afua, a healer who was coming to town at a time when I was really sick. I was broke so I bought the cheapest product offered, the green clay and rubbed it over my cancerous protrusion. To my amazement it disappeared. When I couldn't find her products I turned to Adamah's red clay, which I used internally to remove toxins as instructed. Many co-workers used it with great success after I told them about it.

Dietary laws can be found in ancient documents. I give thanks to Malachi who always pushed a natural diet and raw food. I give thanks to Dr. Sebi for bringing up the fact that you can heal through herbs. He was the first to say the body is electric. He helped Lisa Lopes and many others find the path to health. He cured others of aids, quiet as it is kept. I give thanks to Llaila Africa for teaching about wholeness, thus reviving the African holistic model. And I give thanks to Neetta Black and Mr. Moore for encouraging the publication of this book.

Introduction

The problem with kidney disease is that symptoms are practically non-existent. By the time you discover you have a problem, you kidney could be far gone. Unfortunately there are many who buy into the idea that kidney disease is irreversible.

It has been said that it takes patients four days to recuperate from dialysis. Judging from what I see, that is true. I have seen people nearly fall out of their chair after a treatment. Unable to keep up, they walk around like zombies. My kidney condition was pretty bad. I had high blood pressure, swollen feet, swollen face, swollen organs, a mini-stroke, metallic taste in my mouth, and a scheduled operation. I had dark lumps protruding out that hurt. I could not keep food down. I too walked around like a zombie, barely making it from bed to work. The difference between them and me is that, I think it is never too late.

Whatever your reasons for getting kidney disease, you too, can heal. Those who have not been diagnosed, may have kidney inflammation and not know it. I had it and did not know it until it was too late. Unfortunately kidney disease and high blood pressure can go undetected for a long time because there are no symptoms. The following are hints that you may have kidney issues-dizziness, nausea, edema [swelling ankles, swollen face or in other words, water retention]. You may experience frequent urination or scanty urination. Your urine may be intense in color. It may even burn. There may be other hints depending on which type of kidney issue you have. But either way, people will tell you that kidney dysfunction is irreversible.

They said the same thing about diabetes and cancer.

I am totally convinced that many people did not have to die of kidney dysfunction. Their lives could have been saved with intervention from plants and roots, among other modalities. If anyone dies of kidney complications it is because they do not have the will to live as strong as I. Every day I meet someone who either has kidney problems or knows someone who does. The list is endless. Many have had a kidney transplant already. There is something wrong with this picture. In times past, this was not the case. The cases of kidney infection have increased from the times of our ancestors to now. People used to go in the bushes to get well. Now they go to a butcher - the surgeon.

I had gotten to the point where I was so toxic and constipated, that I hadn't had a bowel movement in what felt like months. My belly protruded. People thought I was pregnant. I was fat even by my own mother's standards. She used to call me skinny all the time. Growing up we were always at war about me not eating.

My people knew about medicinal plants and roots. I grew up watching adults place large herb leaves over people's heads, offer medicinal teas and herbal baths. The very people that nearly exterminated us are the ones we are trusting to cut us up. They ask us what have we done for our symptoms so far. We tell them what herbs we are taking. Then they try to replicate these in labs. These dissected herbs or chemicals produce side effects. I have gone back to old school.

In my search for my roots, I found that our diet is far superior to any foreign diet. Just yucca alone contains a myriad of vitamins and minerals incomparable to the potato. Due to the confusion brought about by slavery, many arts had to go underground, and many people died with their secrets, including healing modalities.

Chapter 1

They Cannot Believe
I Am Still Standing

You could have kidney disease and not know it. The symptoms are very subtle. Our environment is so polluted anyone could have it and not know it. I found out I had kidney disease way after it was much too late. They'll lead you to believe you need dialysis or a transplant. Being the naturalist that I am I went into research mode and interviewed many people. The good news is that kidney function is reversible!

After undergoing several near death experiences, people show disbelief that I am still standing. Yet the medical records speak for themselves. What I did not realize is that when I started writing this book, I was going to open a can of worms. For example, the push for dialysis may be money driven. The many accidents that occur during dialysis go unreported for the most part. Part of it is fear of insurance premiums going up.

I also found out the following. You do not need a license to run a dialysis clinic. Drinking water is full of chemicals that dim our intellect. Population reduction is no accident.

Since we are still plagued with linear thinking, nutrition is not taught in medical school. Thank goodness I turned to alternative treatment. One treats symptoms, the other school of thought treats the individual.

The good news is, after going through self-healing techniques, I found out that there are clinics that employ both conventional and alternative modes of heal ing. Whether you chose one or the other or both, is a personal choice. But before you decide, continue reading so that you may see which tests, analysis and healing methods do what. Sometimes you can benefit from both. Just know that there are many choices.

My healing did not happen over-night. After years of accepting a corrupt eating diet, I became comfortable with it. As a Taurus, I stubbornly clung to it, though my instincts had previously told me otherwise. I reasoned that when in Rome, do as the Romans. In other words, eat what you're served, lest you become a nuisance. I remember days of being the oddball. Somewhere along the way, I lost my way, giving in to the "Romans." In retrospect, it is hard to believe that I almost lost my life. I was the one who wrote the thesis about the drawbacks of meat eating. My classmates chewed me out as they stubbornly clung to an errant lifestyle. Today, I do not judge people for their choices. All I know is that some choices work for some and not others. Meat eating has proven to be difficult to digest.

Meat can have too many chemicals, depending on how the animal was raised. Even vegetarians are bombarded with chemicals if they are not careful. There are chemicals in processed foods, water, the air, and everywhere you turn.

Today we are exposed to radioactive waves more than ever. People used to run from areas heavy-laden with natural radioactivity. Our elders would show us the way, such as where to establish a home. Today we radioactivity is everywhere. This is due to man-made radioactivity, such as electrical wires, computers, microwaves, telephone wires for landlines, cell phones and so on. Evidence is abundant that being exposed to this lifestyle over a period of time does affect you.

I also write about the toxic effect all these chemicals are having on us. My thing is, we did not become toxic over overnight. There are many toxins bombarding our life right now. This could include but is not limited to eating habits, lack of exercise, being exposed to radio-active waves, being exposed to negatrons [negative people], not drinking enough water, holding your urine due to modern lifestyle or being a slave to work. The lifestyle that is created for us causes stress. Gone are the days when you simply claim your piece of land and build your own house.

Ever notice how tired you get when you stay in front of the computer or television? It is not your imagination. Radiation from computers is real.

Chapter 2

How I Found Out
I Had Kidney Disease

I refused to go into dialysis treatment whereas people with twenty percent kidney function were required to go into dialysis. I went as far as voluntarily taking the same test. So yes, after doing what is in this book, my numbers improved dramatically. The numbers include creatine level, cholesterol, glucose, serum, protein, albumin and uric acid.

Just about everyone I run into tells of a relative or friend who went into dialysis at twenty percent function. A person on dialysis was shocked to hear I was still walking around at the five percent kidney function level because she recalls that when it gets down to twenty percent function people are asked to go into dialysis immediately. I believe in the healing power of the body. I fear the side effects of conventional treatment more so than the treatment itself.

Have you ever noticed that when it comes to major conditions, the treatment kills the patient? Chemotherapy is the perfect example. My father died from side effects of a medicine that was supposed to treat his heart. It ruined his liver.

While he was alive he told me of a compatriot who moved to the mountains after living in the United States and given a few months to live. He suffered from cancer. For whatever reason, he benefited from the mountain's fresh air and a diet of strictly spinach. I believe it was the chlorophyll in the spinach that cured him. As for me, I could never go on a spinach diet because oxalates and kidney trouble don't mix. If you have kidney troubles do not ever eat foods with too much oxalates such as spinach and chocolate. So if you're thinking of doing something similar, try cilantro or kale. (**The Natural Pharmacy**, p.284)

Since I am able to keep myself from becoming as sick as the others I am constantly asked what am I doing right. After saying the same thing over and over to many different people, I realize many other people may benefit from this information. What is surprising is the number of people that are actually distressed by serious kidney problems. I found this out after telling people I was doing a book on the subject. It seems to me people are unnecessarily checking out.

My [almost] checking out began with me feeling pain on my right side. No longer able to bear the discomfort, I go to the Emergency Room. To my dismay, I am told my left kidney is inflamed and that I need to be tested for kidney stones. I remind the doctor that the pain is on the right side, not the left. He said sometimes you could go in forone thing and find you have an unrelated problem. The nurse says it could also be displaced pain. I didn't buy it. To this day I don't know why that right pain kept persisting for two years. I told the doctor and nurse that I did have gallbladder problems on the right side before; so severe in fact, that the hospital had scheduled an operation. Somehow three days later I healed [after lots of prayers], I recalled, as I told the story. They both assured me my gallbladder was perfect. After tiring of this conversation I just think to myself, do these people really know what they are talking about? Then I realized it's all for the better. I don't believe in having body parts taken out. Many people that have body parts taken out still have problems.

Then I flashed back to 1992, where the pain was so severe, I practically lived in the ER Room. But, no one could find what was wrong. Little did I know I had several things going on at the same time. The level of toxicity was so subtle; it crept up on me, until one day my body gave out. All kinds of tests were done on me. I even had X-rays and a colonoscopy. A camera was inserted inside my body during this procedure. They look for ulcers, tumors, cysts, blockages, but could find none. After being sent home repeatedly, I remember crying at home on the couch helplessly, unable to move. I felt as though a giant snake was dancing inside my stomach and intestines, growing bigger and bigger. I felt sorry for my husband, who had to get up in the middle of the night to drive me to the

Emergency Room every other day. Eventually, his patience wore out. At times, I would drive myself there, while the ER people didn't know what to think.

That usually happens when they can't figure out what's wrong with you. Ironically, now suddenly they're wondering why I neglected myself and didn't come sooner. I explained the long battle of re-visiting the ER Room and doctors and specialists. I am reminded medicine is not a precise science.

"We are aware that you have been diagnosed with Irritable Bowel Syndrome (IBS)." The ER doctor continues, " but this is inflamed kidney, which is a separate issue." Weakly, I ask, "Are you sure my kidney is inflamed?" A resounding yes came forth from all three doctors and nurses combined. "As sure as the X-ray that were taken", they say. I must have had a disbelief look on my face, because, the X-ray is displayed at this time, and I'm told my kidney is so badly inflamed, I could have kidney stones. I am urged to do a follow up with the primary doctor and a specialist, as I am given a solemn look. At this point, I realize they are serious. I wonder why this wasn't discovered earlier. "Haven't you been having back pain? Fever? They query. "Maybe", came the reply, "but not really noticeable." They cannot believe I didn't have any symptoms. "No, not now, but from 1992 to 1997 I did," "We're not talking about your Irritable Bowel Syndrome," the doctor reminded me, "We are totally aware of that." "What happened between 1997 and 2005 [with IBS]?" I reply, "Nothing." The doctor says, "My point exactly." "You better take care of this if you want to save your kidney."

That was just the beginning. Wait till you hear of the purple lump that was sticking out of me [later] and other bad news. To tell you the truth, I got tired of taking Zantacs for the irritable bowel syndrome and whatever else they were giving me.

Eventually I am examined for a voiding cystogram and everything in between. I am asked if I have a metallic taste in my mouth. I wondered how they knew. Later the urologist asks me if I throw up right after I eat. These people are good. They know exactly what will happen and when. Eventually they schedule a kidney operation. They treat me as though I'm dying going out of their way to make me extremely comfortable. Now looking back I see why. I spent a day at the hospital and don't recall what they did to me. It seems they inserted a tube. My doctor then told me that eventually my kidney might have to come out. "How will I know when?" I asked. The urologist said, "you'll know because you'll become extremely sick." By the way, I also had circulation problems so bad I had heart problems, leg stiffness, and eventually a mini-stroke. I was even asked if I had my will in order, during a heart problem.

So you see, you can have kidney failure and be symptomless. Scary eh? That's why you must take care of your health and reverse whatever damage has already taken place.

Chapter 3

What Causes It?

I follow up with my doctor, whom I trust as one of the most open-minded people in the world. She confirms everything the ER said, and refers me to an urologist. Tests are run. One procedure was almost an operation. A biopsy was scheduled and an operation was supposed to take place. In another procedure, so much took place; I was not allowed to drive myself home.

I asked many questions. "Is this necessary?" I could tell that I was wearing my urologist out. "Don't you trust me?" he seemed to be saying. I was told my kidney only functions at a rate of five percent. "It may have to be removed," he continued solemnly. I asked, "When?" He replies, "You'll know." His answer was shrouded in mystery. Again I asked what the symptoms would be since I had kidney problems all this time and didn't know it. He said, "Just bring yourself to the hospital." "But how would I know if it's infected?" I queried. He said, "Oh, you'll know all right, because, you'll get real sick." "You'll get so sick, you'll have no choice but to come to the hospital. It's going to be that bad." With that kind of statement, I had no choice but to believe him.

Okay, by now it was clear IBS was passé, and kidney disease was well under way. The people at work added stress to an already stressful situation. The attitude was one of disbelief and threats of AWOL. Can you believe the insensitivity? I was harassed for a one-day absence, and for the rest of my illness. I had to bring medical proof over a one-day absence, so you can imagine the treatment when I kept my doctor's appointments. Though it didn't meet the three-day absence requirement, I obliged, showing proof of illness, which they used against me in court by the way. And thus began my battle with the Feds. That's a separate book unto itself.

Everyone is puzzled as to how I winded up with kidney disease, of all things. No one in my family had it. My own mother could not believe I was diagnosed as such. "Are you sure?" she kept asking me. She said, "Tu sabes adonde estan los rinones?" I assured her I knew what rinones were, and where they were located. My co-workers were especially skeptical because to them, I ate so healthy. In fact, they came to me for advise on all kinds of alternative nutrition and alternative therapies. And I had healed many people. They seemed to just know that I knew. Sometimes I wonder if something is written on my forehead that says "healer." I was constantly urged to write books about healing.

During one of my visits to the nurse, I was reminded that I had had bouts with high blood pressure before. "But I was never put medication for it" I protested, "Do you feel dizzy?" she asked. "Yes," came my reply. "Well" she continued, "that's a sign of high blood pressure." I thought it was stress from the toll free line. Either way, the toll free line added to whatever was going on. Additionally, being confined to the telephone and having to explain whereabouts when I go to the restroom did not help. That's how sick the place is. It is bad enough having to endured to endure holding one's urine as a caregiver at daycare, as a schoolteacher and now as a toll-free operator. Even as a retail clothing salesperson, supervisors wondered where I was, when I would go to the restroom. They suspect you if you go often as if people have time to play games. I got fired from the retail store. They could care less what chronic illness I had. This is all the more reason to start my own business. I was tired of the job stress and pressure. I had enough going on with inheritances that never manifested and didn't need the silly games at work from people trying to score brownie points.

The boss at the Feds was still on my trail about going to the bathroom, while I was supposed to be on the phone. I had had urinary track infections before, but other bosses weren't quite as mean. Eventually I had a Trans-Ischemic-Attack, mini-stroke, which wasn't so mini. The Feds trivialized it in court. I had physical therapy and my face was contorted. For a long time I couldn't drive or feed myself. I lost weight but the Feds didn't care. They harassed my doctors. This explains why some doctors don't like to participate in EEO or federal cases. Even lawyers will tell on other lawyers, and how they fear the IRS. They play dirty. I was absent for a long time after the stroke. After being coerced to return prematurely he assaults me sexually. I was so messed up from the stroke I couldn't defend myself very well. I was absent even more after that. I lost two houses and one business. The Feds took after each other and engaged in a big cover up. In fact, I never got all of my transcripts. That was deliberate because the witnesses were too powerful. He had done it to so many people. But some of the witnesses were fired shortly after the ordeal. They made sure they cleaned up their mess. The police appeared to be in on it.

They kept the whole thing hush-hush. But when their people had ministrokes of a lesser degree they announced it to everyone begging for pity. The gap between the haves and have-nots is staggering. That is why I dedicate my book to the disenfranchised.

People that knew my healthy eating habits were even more baffled when they found out about the mini-stroke. "You eat so healthy!" they insisted. I agreed with everyone. I hope the stress from the job didn't have me visiting the vending machine too much. My regular doctor told me I had too much protein in my urine. That right there made me suspect meat to be the culprit. After a dream where a fish was telling me "don't eat me! please!" a doctor told me to stay way from meat. He said especially stay away from chicken, salt, sugar, dairy products and especially eggs. And not too long afterwards, there was a mercury scare on TV regarding fish.

The pills that the alternative doctor gave me worked, but the symptoms would return as soon as I stopped taking them. Another Chinese doctor gave me tea to ingest. But I felt the healing was too slow and there had to be more to it when you are as advanced in disease as I was. My primary doctor told me to stay away from alcohol. But the pills she gave me just did not agree with my body. When she prescribed pharmaceuticals, I took them at first, until I started having side effects that were not pretty. They constricted blood from going to my brain. I was moving in slow motion. I was so drugged up from kidney medicine and stroke medicine. This slowing down effect led them to think it was mental issues. Since the medicine made me move slow and since I was traumatized from the sexual battery at work that took place right after the mini-stroke, I was given anti-depressants with the assurance that it was NOT for any emotional issues; only to prevent heart problems from repeating. This made me move even slower. Then I am pressured to return to work, or else I would be given AWOL. The perpetrator knew it was standard procedure, but he presented it with a devilish twist to it, because some people are simply evil.

I had to eventually fake feeling better just to remain employed and pay bills. There were others also who confessed faking feeling better just to keep the job, particularly a single Mom and an elderly guy. This helps to keep food on the table. You'd be surprised to find out just how bad I felt.

The thing with the Feds is, they are so wicked. If you feel bad, it's your fault. So you see? They do anything to keep from being accountable. They hate paying worker's compensation, though we are the ones paying into the system. If you forget something they blame the stroke. If you remember something they accuse you of not having a stroke at all. You would think they went to medical school the way they're constantly diagnosing people.

My stomach was protruding so much people constantly asked me if I was pregnant. I was no longer digesting food at all. In fact, I would even throw up seconds after eating. I even asked myself if I was pregnant. I took a pregnancy test so frequently it wasn't funny. Later I developed a lumpy dark patch that protruded out of my skin. It was hard and made me feel uncomfortable. I tried Queen Afua's healing clay and the cancerous purple protruding, painful lump disappeared. The doctors couldn't find anything in particular. My "stomach" hurt all the time. Since this has gone on since 1993, I was convinced no doctor could help me. I was destined to cure myself through alternative methods. It was along this thinking that I decided dialysis was not for me. If I die in the process, oh well. We all have to go sometime. But I am not going to offer myself as a guinea pig and die prematurely.

Nutrition Blockage

At some point I realized I was beyond the point of no return. No matter how much I ate, I was hungry all the time. What I learned later is that you cannot nourish a body that is toxic. If the blood has been compromised, you have to clean up the blood before the body would accept nutrients. So eating period, no matter how healthy I ate, was a waste of time. Once I realized this, I began to purify my blood. In another chapter I speak of how I got rid of toxins. If you feel tired all the time you might be experiencing nutrition blockage. No matter what a person eats, or how powerful the supplements, it is a waste of time to take them if a person is toxic. This can happen if food won't digest or if a person is constipated. When people are full of chemicals and heavy metals, they may not absorb vitamins and minerals.

Antibiotics

At first, I had no idea that tonsillitis and commercial antibiotics can ruin the kidneys. So, you see, there can be so many different causes, just like with any other disease. A long time ago I also took antibiotics for strep throat. It has been proven that antibiotics contribute in a deadly way to lead to kidney disease. (**African Holistic Healing**)

It would take a book to include the damages that long-term antibiotics cause. Doctors are the first to admit that antibiotic use period can be damaging. So why do we do it? Many people are not aware that there are natural antibiotics as alternatives. Oregano and Echinacea are natural antibiotics to name a few.

The worker compensation people love it because they don't have to pay you when they aggravate your condition, although technically they are required to. Where we work, it was known that people had an unusual level of kidney disease compared to the rest of the population. Even though the guidelines clearly say, "if the condition is aggravate, the employer is liable" they ignored it each time. This is what I call bully employers.

Over the Counter Drugs

One doctor told me that NSAIDs can affect the kidneys. I did take these pharmaceuticals for inflammation when I was having hypertension just before the ER visit. Another source stated that Non-Stroidal Anti-Inflammatory Drugs cause kidney stones. He stated that some sources of NSAIDs are aspirin, motrin, Advil, Naproxen and Aleve. I took Naproxen for inflammation. Coming from two reliable professional sources, how can you argue with that? (**The Natural Pharmacy**)

Supposedly "Heredity"

I really don't believe that people inherit disease per se. And then again, I do. So it's a matter of what you mean by inheriting disease. The trouble with the idea of inheriting disease is that people take on a fatalistic attitude and give up trying to beat the odds blaming it on uncontrollable genes. Hogwash. Even if your parents ate bad and passed on disease to you, you can still reverse disease.

Can doctors tell if a child is born with inherited kidney problems? If a child has puffy eyes or some other sign of inflammation does this mean the Mom ate too much salt during pregnancy? Does this mean the mother held her urine during pregnancy? One thing is for sure, anyone who holds their urine will have compromised their kidney.

Not Urinating Frequently Enough

Many people hold their urine because they are in a work situation. That was certainly the case with me. Every job I held required holding your urine. I worked in daycare centers, as a teacher and finally as a customer service representative on a toll free line. We were monitored so carefully until we were made to explain every time we were away from our desk, including using the bathroom time. For this reason, I wrote the poem, "Are Jobs Worth Having/Work For Self" And, of course, there were the stooges at work who support the scrooge, the Uncle Toms and Willy Lynchers who add stress to an already stressful situation. People whose lifestyles are not that bad, yet manifest kidney problems is usually for one of two reasons; either they are stressed or don't use the bathroom enough. The more I think about it, the more I think it was the latter in my situation. I grew up eating sensible breakfasts, but then strayed from the mother diet and lifestyle in general. In our country you eat the big meal at noon. We did not eat after 7pm. The last meal is light and eaten at 6 pm. Everyone was asleep around 8:30pm. And you better not get caught awoke around 10:00

pm. All this changes when you move to America. The work schedule simply does not allow for this; whereas in Latin America, people are given a two-hour lunch in order that people go home and eat their dinner with their family. You can even take a nap and then return to work.

But in America people have to drink coffee to fight off the sleep that comes naturally at mid-day. The American's version of dinner is held as supper in our countries. We eat a light supper. This way, the digestive system is not exhausted. If Americans want to lose weight, they would follow suit. It is not just a weight issue. It is a health issue. Fecal matter lying overnight when the body is supposed to be at rest is a very uncomfortable position to be in. You do not sleep well. It's a losing battle for your digestive system. It's bad enough that we don't digest food after 7:00 pm, but then to try and force the body to digest what takes four hours to digest is a lot to ask the body to do.

Eating Meat

Meat takes at least four hours to digest. No wonder we are sick! There are those who insist it takes four days. But whether it's four hours or four days, it still is longer than anything you will ever eat. Keep in mind that the kidneys are the part of the filtering system. Any doctor can tell you that people with kidney problems have high amounts of protein in their blood. (**The Natural Pharmacy** p284, **The PH Miracle** 158,). Even adult onset diabetes is diet related.(**Alternative Medicine** p 537)

A Body That Is Too Acid

When the body is too acid, we become sick. It is that simple. People who eat meat, dairy products, processed sugar and processed flour are bound to be too acidic. To get the body in a healthy state, a state of alkalinity, one must eat more fruits and vegetables.

Many people think lemons cause the body to be acid, because it has an "acid" taste. Nothing could be further from the truth! Lemons have one of the highest alkaline states there is. Lemon is the ultimate disease fighter!

Honey makes your saliva alkaline, if eaten straight from the honeycomb. You would think people would stop eating things that make them sick. Unfortunately, though, we're dealing with addictions or habits, some of which are tied to emotions.

Stress

Although modernity has made our lives easier in some ways, we have more stress than ever. Never before have we had to respond to so many stimuli. We are doing things that our ancestors never had to do. We pay numerous bills. Everything has a price. Things that used to be free are no longer. We pay for water and sometimes oxygen. We pay rent and other utilities. We listen to the news, watch TV, and listen to the radio. We use computers for work, for recreational communication, recreational activities and for other activities. Because of us having to pay for free stuff, we stay away from our families, including children. This causes more stress as we work harder in order to provide. The very people that we are trying to make happier, we are making them unhappy by not being around.

We feel compelled to buy things we normally wouldn't, so the kids won't feel left out. For example, we may let them participate in sports. Sometimes it's more than trying to establish a sense of belonging. Sometimes we do it to keep them off the street or out of trouble, while we are away, at work, of course. Sometimes our parents live in another state or another household. The extended family of African peoples is no longer extended.

Indigenous people used to breast-feed their babies. This created a bond. If that bond is broken, or never established, children do not learn as well. Their brains shrink. That has been scientifically proven. We worry about money for college as our lives are taxed away. We are bombarded with radioactive waves, microwaves, telephone lines, cell stations, cell phones waves, and X-rays. Doctors warn you about X-rays. You are told not to be around X-rays unless absolutely necessary. One doctor told a group of us not to take X-rays unless we are far gone, because of the dangers of it. Never before have people been surrounded by so many wires.

High Blood Pressure

I must start out with a disclaimer about this section. I'm getting ready to tell you how to get off high blood pressure medicine. The disclaimer is this. I am not a doctor, so you must stay on your high blood pressure medicine until you wean yourself out slowly. The reason is this; if high blood pressure goes unchecked, you could bust your capillaries. So it is better to take your conventional medications than not to take anything at all. Think about it. The brain has a lot of capillaries, so do the legs portions and so do the kidneys. Notice that people's legs get chopped when they're diabetic. The kidneys go dysfunctional. The brain gets a stroke. All of this is associated with high blood pressure and capillaries. When you have high blood pressure, you are at risk of losing those parts of your bodies that have lots of capillaries. So, you would do well to take your high blood pressure medicine, unless of course, you have an alternative. But you must stick with the alternative for it to be effective just as you would your medicine.

High blood pressure is something that needs to be addressed as soon as it is discovered. When left unchecked, high blood pressure can lead to kidney dysfunction. High blood pressure is known as the silent killer because it creeps up on you with very little symptoms if any. Others may notice dizziness in the advanced stages. The question is why are so many people suddenly having this problem? The answer could be diet or stress. We know stress can destroy someone's physical body. In a like manner, eating the wrong foods can stress the body physically, to the point where the circulatory system is out of control. Many people are under the impression that they have to be on medication for the rest of their life. That is simply not true. It certainly helps doctors who need to pay their medical bills.

But what are the side effects of these pharmaceuticals? Some interfere with sleep. Others make you drowsy. I personally was moving in slow motion so I was ready to get off medication. You can use olive leaf to get your pressure back to normal. It is one of the most potent alternatives out there. They come in leaf form at Mutana in West End Georgia. You may also get it in pill form at your local health food stores. You may also use brown algae for the same purpose. People who take brown algae consistently eventually get off medications completely. The trick is being consistent. You must be consistent.

Some people give up taking products as soon as they start to feel better. I tend to do that but then it just prolongs symptoms. In other words, it makes healing drag on. Disciplined people, can do it in less time. Olive leaf is very potent. When I buy it in pill form I open the capsule, place it under my tongue and swallow with liquid such as lemonade. Others can just boil the dry leaves. The powdered pills can be found at various health food stores such as the one found next to La Fitness on Sugarloaf in Duluth or Lawrenceville area. I would suggest Life's Essential because they have everything. They are located in West End Cascade area. They also sell herbs in bulk.

Quercetine helps high blood pressure and even stroke symptoms. You can find it in red onions. The Indians were well aware of it.

Anyone suffering from high blood pressure should eliminate table salt altogether. It is a poison. Instead, people should try the miracle salt otherwise known as Himalayan salt. Back in the day, it was known as a very expensive commodity. You actually were paid in salt because its healing value was well recognized. Think of all the minerals in salt and how the body naturally contains these minerals.

The great Teacher once said "I am salt." He also said "Ye are the salt of the Earth." In a vision I was asked, "What is the chemical composition of salt?" It was not a multiple-choice question. I was expected to research for the answer. One Master once told me dreams are sometimes meant just for you. So perhaps I needed that message because of how my body was suffering.

The book is designed to save the people in the shortest amount of time. We are facing an epidemic of high proportion. No other time in history has there been such staggering statistics. The percentage of kidney disease just continues to escalate like a cancer. How to you go from thousands into the millions in less than twenty years? There is something wrong with this picture. Why the sudden increase in kidney disease? What are we doing differently? We are more stressed because our resources keep being taken away. We are now paying for what is free to every living species across the world - land and water. Some pay for oxygen at oxygen cafes. Demons say do this, "eat day and night" and out of season, "follow the food pyramid" and other lies. We follow like sheep being led to the slaughterhouses. The sudden epidemic owes its spread to other things like corn syrup being put in every food form. (Video – see appendix, **Natural Cures**)

It owes its growth to the fluoride and chlorine being put in water. **(Cancer And Nutrition).** If all these assaults on the body don't give you high blood pressure something else will. So the key is knowing how to avoid what "everybody else" is doing.

Heavy Metals

One reason we are not functioning at brain capacity is because of the fluoride that is put in the water. Did you know that fluoride makes you dumb? **(The Boston Globe July 2005 on autism**). The placement of fluoride in water is designed to dumb you down. Cadmium tends to do the same thing. This is what you find in vaccines as well. Since most people have been dumbed down, it is best not to be surprised at their initial reaction. Some shrug their shoulders and say everything is dangerous. That is a very fatalistic reaction. To resign yourself to whatever is given to you or forced upon you is unacceptable. Obtaining a home filter for the entire house is a solution. Some have reported great success with this method. There is a superior filter. The mother of all filters is the wellness filter www.wellnessfilter.com. You can put it in your kitchen, your shower or throughout the entire house. The latter is preferable since the skin absorbs everything. Think about it, when you shower your skin takes in all the chemicals in that shower water. This includes chlorine, fluoride, cadmium, arsenic and whatever else they decide to put in the water.

Staying In Touch With Your Feelings

There is nothing wrong with listening to authority, except when they are wrong. People trust doctors and teachers though these same people were trained by the very system that oppresses them. It is important to stay stress free. Play soft music, and think progressively. All diseases originate in the mind. Be mindful of your thoughts.

Eating too much or too little could be the result of a distorted mind or a mind that has been wounded. The same is true for people who eat the wrong foods. Anything that makes you hurt when you eat it can be the result of an allergic reaction. This allergic reaction could manifest in the form of a headache or stomachache. Some people take their chances on peanuts, wheat products, milk products and tomatoes. Many people have allergies to these foods and don't know it. Some over-eat or don't eat when they're nervous or sad. People must stay in touch with their feelings and their bodies. Eating when you're not hungry can throw your body out of whack. Because we are sociable beings we eat when others eat - whether at luncheons, social gatherings or just because it's there. Control of your body is the key to balance.

Electromagnetic Waves

As stated above, we are exposed to electromagnetic waves like never before. In ancient times, the elders led villages to areas that were safe for establishing an abode. This was all done in an effort to avoid natural Earth radioactivity. If natural radioactivity is bad for you, imagine what man-made radioactivity does to you. Anyone who watches TV over a period of time knows what I am talking about. You begin to feel drained. The same can be said of people who are forced to work in front of computers. People who voluntarily use a computer for a long time experience this drainage. You can use tourmaline stones and cedar bark powder to counteract this. Microwaves were prohibited to us for a reason. Microwaves emit such strong rays that they kill living organisms. So in essence, you are eating dead foods.

Cell phone usage has its limitations. I sometimes wonder if the people that put on studies and TV commercials about how cell phones are not harmful are connected to the sale of cell phones. It is hard to ignore the uncomfortable pulling effect one feels when engaged in cell phone usage. Face it - we are electrical beings. (Dr Sebi). Everything is made up of electrons, neutrons and atoms. We are magnetic beings. It should not surprise anyone to find out that we are moved by magnetic waves. There is usually a conflict of interest when reports suddenly change from before. Now they're saying cell phones do not cause brain tumors despite all the other correlative studies. For some people, no study is necessary. Depending on how primitive their phone is they feel a pull when they put the phone to the ear. Some people find relief in using earplugs. A publication on protective devices is forthcoming.

MRI's, which stand for magnetic resonance imaging systems, also produce electromagnetic waves. Lord knows I had my share of MRI's after the kidney situation was discovered. MRI's expose one to electromagnetic radiation. Atoms resonate at certain frequencies. It is not clear whether MRI's interfere with the frequency of atom resonation. But one thing is for sure. Too much of it is no good. The very doctors that work with these machines are the first to tell you that [if you ask]. Better still, look it up in any medical journal.

Today's Music

Today's music can be anything but soothing. Music used to be harmonious. You do not need a Master's degree in music to notice something is off key or too high to be a regular note. Yet professional musicians will tell you that the musical scale has been changed. What used to be a specific note has moved up the scale. The music is Satanic. The powers that be, or demonic agents, deliberately follow suit, to keep you off track. This is part of the distraction so you won't know what is really happening. If you really ponder it, you come to know.

Propaganda Bombardment

Propaganda is part of an ulterior. The TV is the perfect vehicle. Television watching can make one feel inadequate - not rich enough, not beautiful enough, not skinny enough or whatever. (Naomi Judd **Aging Gracefully**.)

Not only do we spend precious years of our lives watching whatever, but also TV demoralizes one and focuses on violence. The increase in violence has been linked to TV over and over again. Furthermore, we could be more productive if we watch less TV. You could start your own business or be more creative. Start a hobby.

When we were little, we went outside. We played with rocks, and sticks. We made houses, and furniture. We were creative. Being left without TV forces one to use their imagination, inventiveness, and creativity. As children, we played cowboys and girls. We even made houses with sticks. I remember all the neighborhood children would come and play with us due to our creativity and unusual games. We pretended to be other people and played various guessing games, which involved jumping and running. Today's children and teenagers are saying, "Entertain me." I'm bored," as if it is your job to entertain children. Whatever happened to inventiveness and going swimming?

Television makes you more materialistic. It also serves as a vehicle by which to dis-inform you. It comes in the form of entertainment. The captive audience - you, are not even aware that you are being lectured to or brainwashed. When TV first came out, there was a movie with Gene Kelly and Judy Garland. It was about the war and Gene being caught up in love and trying to prove that he was not a coward. The more I watched it, the more I became convinced that it was a very clever propaganda to get boys and men to enlist in the war. Later they started glamorizing cigarette smoking and drinking. The profit motif is obvious. But what is not so obvious is that all these distractions are by design and they really are trying to kill us with this stuff. This brings me to cigarette smoking and alcohol.

Cigarette Smoking and Alcohol

Cigarette smoking is encouraged in the media until recently. Concerned citizens protested. Same thing happened with drinking. Dean Martin, Sammy Davis Jr. and Frank Sinatra were especially used as vehicles to promote alcoholic beverage drinking. They all drank and smoked on national television except Dean Martin who faked the drinking part. Whatever the story, the point is that bad habits were being glamorized. Cigarette contains formaldehyde, cyanide, lead, arsenic, and rat poison among other things. (**Cancer and Nutrition**). Nicotine stains the teeth and coats your lungs. Even if you are not a smoker, this can affect you if someone in your family smokes, or even a co-worker. When you step outside your job for fresh air during breaks or just to go home period, you encounter smokers who leave a bad odor behind. You ingest this nasty stuff through no will of your own. So having designated smoke areas does not help because you still have to get in and out of the building. And smokers are everywhere. They are in the front, the back and on the sides. You even find them in the parking lot.

Alcoholic beverages are a choice. But there are substances that contain alcohol that you would never guess. The best bet is to read the label. Homeopathy medicine contains alcohol. So do cough medicines and some health tonics. It still affects your brain. How you think, how you speak. Know what you are doing. This stuff will eat your teeth. Perhaps it is the sugar content or a combination of sugar and alcohol. If you already have kidney problems for whatever reasons, taking formaldehyde, cadmium and lead certainly won't help.

As a matter of fact, many people with kidney problems are full of radioactive chemicals. (**<u>Good Health For African Americans</u>**) When you go on dialysis they try to draw out these heavy metals and clean your blood. It's always better to do it the natural way. No machine can act as your filter like your body can. Number one, you'll be on a machine forever. Imagine the money that comes out of your pocket. Also, you get drained once all of your blood comes out and it's placed in the machine. Your blood comes out of your body to be cleaned or "filtered." Number two, who wants to be a dependent? Just get your kidney to function and be through with it.

Seaweed and selenium are ways to get heavy metals out of your system.

Some Ways to De-Stress

It may be helpful for some people to get themselves hipnotized. Others might benefit by listening to motivational tapes or a speaker. Another thing you can do is use affirmations to de-stress. I would use affirmations like "I will win the battle of evil," by making the beginning letters my password; IWWTBOE. In this way, I was forced to listen to this mantra everyday.

Too Much Sugar

We put on pounds of non-foods in our system, disguised as food, and then we wonder what causes the malfunction. We abuse our bodies with items that have zero nutritional values and then wonder why we are sick. What is the vitamin content of a cup of coffee? What value of nutrition can you get out of table salt or fried chips? How about chocolate bars loaded with sugar? When are we going to realize that sugar robs us of our vitamins? Sugar is responsible for bone loss. When are we going to realize that parasites thrive on sugar and rotted flesh [meat]? My mother used to always tell me that eating sugar causes parasites to live inside you. She said they begin to eat your nourishment and you become malnourished. Now I marvel at how much our ancestors knew.

Over-Eating

Social eating is when people eat not because they are hungry, but because they see other people eating. Sometimes we don't want to offend anybody. So we accept dishes that we would otherwise turn down. In both instances, you only hurt yourself so stop it.

Eating when you are not hungry stretches your stomach and intestines. The result is the tire effect. In addition, indigestion sets in because the body cannot digest as quickly as you can eat. (**Alternative Medicine** p317). When you put food in your system before it has had a chance to digest, the vicious cycle sets in. (radio personality and Nutritionist – Adamah; www.adamahspeaks.com). Indigestion is followed by constipation, which is followed by nutrient mal-absorption, which is followed by indigestion, constipation, mal-absorption and so on. Forget super-sizing and all you can eat buffet. They are nothing but stomach stretchers. Eventually you'll find yourself needing a colonic to get back on track. It is good to get a colonic with the idea that you will not fall into the trap of putting bad items back in your system.

Denatured Flour, Sugar, Meat

Did you know that denatured flour, sugar and meat cause skin discoloration? Did you know that meat could cause insanity? Think mad cow disease. (http://themeatrixx1.com). That's just one condition that has been revealed. Lack of vegetation in cold areas meant some people were deprived of certain vitamins and minerals. Salt was particularly scarce. They did not have the real salt available to them and disease ensued. Real salt is pink and laden with nutrition.

What a co-incidence that people with kidney disease have too much protein in their urine. (**Alternative Medicine** p537). Where do you think the protein comes from? Vegetables have protein amounts, but you could never overdose of protein from vegetables.

One day I got tired of the resurrection routine and decided to get my life together. But it took two years and a half of research and doings. What people don't realize is that pale skin is a state of lack; a condition of lack of melanin that can be pretty detrimental to health. We need melanin to sleep. Sleep is essential to health. Melanin and serotonin go hand in hand.

Today you find people who stop eating meat have better disposition than those who still eat meat. It's bad enough you have to disinfect the counter-tops when uncooked meat is placed upon it. Aside from exposing oneself to the potential of being infected with e.coli and contracting mad cow disease, some people want to eat raw meat. That is the plight of those who insist on eating rare meat.

My beef against meat is that you have to deal with e. coli and mad cow disease to name a few inconveniences. When I was in college, I did a speech on leaving meat alone. I caught some slack. But I stuck to my guns. I had no idea there were so many meat lovers out there. It didn't matter that I quoted what went on in the slaughterhouses. Nor did it matter that animals were not allowed to roam free. No one cared that animals were fed hormones. It is common knowledge that animals that are raised for food production are treated with cruelty. The cages they are put in are so tiny that they cannot turn around. Imagine an animal going to the bathroom in this state. It kind of reminds us of the slaves that were packed like sardines and had to therefore defecate and urinate on themselves and each other.

We don't like to talk about ugly things. But let's face it, ugly things do happen. The way we eat is all relevant. Constipation is relevant. Meat will constipate you before vegetables would. How you smell has to do with how much meat and dairy you eat.

Meat and dairy products have zero fiber. The only cholesterol that is bad is animal cholesterol. All other cholesterols are good for you. There is nothing harmful about coconut oil or palm oil. It is time to bust the myths. Sick animals are used for hamburgers and hot dogs because the FDA does not stop one from doing this. The tradition of cutting up a chicken started out because the chicken had rotting parts, so they cut out the rotted part so you won't see it. Think about that the next time you see cut up chicken. Best to buy the whole chicken if you must eat chicken. At least you'll know what's there. Some countries refuse to eat American food for all these reasons. The trend toward veggie burgers is related to the demand by conscious people to stop being cruel to animals. Some people will run over a squirrel and think nothing of it. These people are not human.

When I did my report and made a speech no one wanted to admit the link between flesh consumption and obesity along with life threatening illnesses. That was twenty-four years ago! Now, I don't push meat or a vegetarian diet. We were given free will so each person has to decide for himself or herself what is best for them. But you might want to know that according to *Veg For Life* organization, vegetarians have 30 percent lower risk of death from heart disease, and they outlive carnivorous people by six years. Now I'm going to quote this organization's literature so you won't think it's just me imagining this.

Raising animals for food is directly linked to massive environmental destruction and resource depletion. The EPA reports that U.S. factory farms produce 350 million tons of manure each year, polluting thousands of miles of rivers and lakes, and contaminating groundwater in 17 states. Every year, tens of thousands of wild animals are trapped, poisoned, shot, and even burned alive in government-sponsored "predator-control" programs because the meat industry claims these animals interfere with grazing farmed animals. valuable water and land resources are squandered for meat production, despite scientific reports stating that the planet's 800 million malnourished people could be fed if these resources were used to produce plant foods.

So the destructive trend continues, as we watch where the priorities are. The website, for those who are interested is www.vegforlife.org. To find out more on what goes on at slaughter- houses do a computer search on meat processing or slaughterhouses or how animals are fed prior to being slaughtered. If you have a soul, you'll never be the same again. In some cases it really doesn't matter that the animals are grass fed. When my brother died, we bought fried chicken from a fast food place for the people. The next day when we tried to eat it there were small white maggots crawling all over it. If this happens when food stays out, imagine what happens in your stomach, where it is warm. My sister never forgot when I told her to stop eating pork. She would never listen. Then one day, worms were crawling from the pork meat out the refrigerator/freezer. She told me that she thought the worms were a sign from God for her not listening to me. She told me that story several times and she never forgot. Neither did I. Needless to say she never ate pork again.

Then I read African Holistic Health by Dr. Llaia O Africa. It was then that I found out I was in good company. He talks about the African Model and the European Model. Europeans created a limited diet and manufactured hunger. The disease beriberi was really running rampant when they implemented the monoculture of sugar cane.

Today some people don't even know what real sugar looks like. I found this to be disturbing, because real sugar has minerals and trace elements. In fact, people who eat sugar cane plant show health improvement. Real sugar cane plant looks like a bamboo plant. While the inside looks white, once extracted, it looks brown due to the molasses and iron content. So it depends on the state the plant is in when you buy it. Some people think sugar is white powder like you see in the commercialized grocery stores. They are shocked when I bring real sugar to work, from the Latin American supermarkets. I am not talking about "brown sugar" which is nothing but processed sugar [de-mineralized] with molasses added to it. Nor am I talking about turbinado sugar, although that is a step up. You'll find real sugar in Latin supermarkets. By the way, I don't use white sugar because it has zero nutritional value. Secondly, it is a poison. And number three; it is processed with pig's blood.

So Dr. Llaila Africa goes on to talk about how Europeans created a mono-crop system, like with cotton. **(African Holistic Healing)**. Many people developed pellagra after experiencing chronic hunger for specific vitamins, minerals and proteins. This produces a deranged appetite that can lead to fatigue and depression. The system created the working class peasants. Africans think abundance for all. Europeans think "lack," or "there is not enough." This way of thinking probably stems from the land they lived in, which provided little vegetation. Thus they became "meat and potato" type of people. Monoculture led to soil erosion. They did not rotate the crops. "They rape the land," mess it up" and curse it," says Dr Llaila Africa. The invasion of Africa, lack of knowledge of food science, and a constipating diet were their significant contributions. For further information see African Holistic Healing by LLaila Africa. The powers that be, add chemicals as additives to foods. Thus our bodies become toxic. Some things just don't mix. But we find ourselves facing lead, cadmium, arsenic and other heavy metals as we are bombarded daily with a lifestyle imposed on us by a condition of lack. The lack of vegetation in Europe led the Europeans to create a system called colonialism, where others do the toil for them. The people in hot climates understood the power of the sun. The sun gives life to plants. The sun heals people. Our ancestors understood the science of the sun. But some who did not understand labeled them sun worshippers.

The people of Haiti understood the kundalini principle and they were labeled snake worshippers. The Black Egyptians understood this as well and they were labeled ungodly. Yet the medical establishment does the same thing with the staff and snake, using it as a symbol of health.

For some reason somebody missed some of the ancient medical texts. This is why we are injected with so many chemicals. But there are other reasons. Some of it has to do with greed. This is why you see them distributing the inferior products to Black neighborhoods. Go to all black neighborhoods and see for yourself. Then, do the same with upscale all white neighborhoods. You will not find inferior stores in these affluent neighborhoods. There is a clear double standard. But even in the affluent neighborhoods, you still have to contend with chemical ridden foods. You'll find anything from antifreeze, to paint thinner as food additives. I cannot even begin to scratch the surface. But if you study the consequences of food additives, you'll understand why there are serial killers, psychopaths, depressed people, chronically ill people and addicts.

I would start by getting rid of all the poisons from my cabinet. This would include white sugar, table salt and white flour. That is exactly how I started on my way to better health. I peeled off the layers as I went, getting rid of foods with monosodium glutamate. Then I would cut down on other things, perhaps using transitional foods here and there. Of course I also tried natural cures to help my body in healing.

But we have gotten away from natural cures. Today many people are paying with their lives due to synthetic poisonings. I wrote the Miseducated Consumer to bring attention to the fact that we don't read labels and we should. There is no reason to ingest something grown in a laboratory. One company has gone as far as growing "chickens" laboratory style. In fact, they are not really chickens. The company is not even allowed to call it chicken. You do not know how far these people will go to get into your pocket. Look at how many trees this being have chopped down in the short time he has been in power. Look at all the lakes he has polluted since he has been in power. It doesn't stop with rivers and oceans; there is the air, too. And why is it that when other indigenous peoples were ruling, this was not the case?

When Blacks and indigenous peoples ruled, they worked around the environment, not against it. You must start to cure, if you are going to fight a spiritual battle. It starts with your diet.

There are edible plants and there are medicinal plants. The fruit of the plant according to the Bible is for your meat. It did not say animals. That whole concept of eating flesh did not begin until after the flood. Today we learn that eating meat is directly related to kidney failure. We later learn that meat and potato is a bad mix. Food combinations are an issue related to the digestion span. Since certain foods take longer to digest than others, they really should not be eaten together. It causes the body to overwork itself, adding extra gastric juices. Thus, whatever got digested first, is not incorporated as nutrient. Whatever nutrients are in a certain food is not absorbed because the digestive system is busy producing gastric juices, thus bypassing nutrient absorption.

Many studies have been conducted that link meat-eating to cancer of the gut or colon, pancreas, gallbladder, and now, even the kidneys. The highest incidence of cancer exists in English speaking countries and Western Europe. The lowest rate of colon cancer appears in Africa, South America and Asia. In South America, the exceptions are two countries, Uruguay and Argentina. Interesting is the fact that both these countries house people of European descent and they practice meat-eating in great quantities. These people's diet coincides with their lifestyles as vaqueros, which is a cow-herding lifestyle or what you might call cowboys. Animal fat diets create a chemical called sterol, creating bile acids in the intestines. In turn, carcinogenic estrogens are produced. The kidneys play a role in processing since they are the body's filters. The liver is a filter as well. The kidney, being a filter, is affected by what you ingest. You tax the system when you overload it with carcinogens and heavy metals. Polyunsaturated fats create a chemical called cholesterol epoxide. Rice eating societies do not have a high cancer rate, whereas beef eating societies do. So do those that depend on milk, eggs, butter and other dairy products. Japanese include a lot of vegetables in their diets. They have a very low rate of cancer. However, Japanese who come to America and eat like Americans show a compromised health. The same is true for young Japanese Americans living in Japan who adopt the American diet. Within only one generation, all the healthy foods the ancestors ate goes out the window. The same is true for any other group. People who eat large amounts of meat usually have no room for healthy foods. Thus, they create a cycle of high fat low fiber ingestion. Those who eat high fiber diets find meat to be too heavy. They appear to be in tune with their bodies and nature. So they notice it takes meat a long time to digest. No one has to tell them this. They display a low incidence of disease. Perhaps it has to do with the fact that the fiber pushes out whatever toxin may exist. What you eat determines what type of bacteria is in you. People who eat a high concentration of vegetables have aerobic types of bacteria. Those who eat dead things like animals portray anaerobic bacteria. Anaerobic bacteria do not need air or oxygen to exist. Bacteria called streptozotocin cause renal cancer. Are you kidney sufferers convinced yet? Beef bile acids travel down the gut and are converted to carcinogens. What is your source of fat? Is your source of fat, animal fat, milk, cheese, eggs or cream? Is your source of fat, coconut oil, coconut cream, palm oil, olive oil, sesame oil, flax seed oil or olives? The ratio of oil to water is crucial. Then, the type of fat is something that needs to be taken into consideration. Do you eat avocados? That is a good source of good fat. Everybody needs fat, but people get confused as to what type. Some people eliminate fat period thinking they are doing the body a favor. Instead, they are causing harm. Everyone needs some type of omega fat. Some people get it from salmon. But those who do not believe in killing life forms or eating flesh will get their source of fat from the aforementioned [olive, flax, etc]. Many different studies involving different ethnic groups target group stools. In each case, it shows that bile acids and meat-eating go hand in hand, just as disease does.

It is bad enough that meat eating produces certain carcinogens. But sometimes what the cows eat make the problem even more complex. Cow's milk consumption by humans has been linked to cancer in humans. Contaminants have been found in milk. Another thing that has been found in cow's milk is heavy metals. (**Cancer and Nutrition**, the meatrix1.com, **African Holistic Healing.**) So now we see that there are many ways to get heavy metals inside you. Some have found DES [diethylstilbestrol] in the past, in milk. Europeans and their descendants continue to have lactase in their system long after babyhood. Other ethnic groups do not. This makes other people lactose intolerant. Americans with European descent have the same enzyme.

Pace of Eating

Eating too fast is an issue. Food cannot be properly digested if it is eaten quickly. The slower you eat and the more you chew what you do have in your mouth, the more weight you will lose. Also, you should not swallow and eat at the same time. This means you should not drink anything while you eat. Many people get hiccups this way. Do not confuse the body trying to get it to perform more than one function at a time.

Not Eliminating During the Elimination Period

Other destructive issues and habits include eating during the elimination period as taught by sister Adamah, the nutritionist, and eating out of season. Not to mention eating genetically engineered foods. The majority of fruits and vegetables we see in regular grocery stores are genetically engineered. You can tell, because the seeds have been removed. This is very dangerous. This further explains why we eat and stay hungry. So that not only are you hungry because you are toxic, but you are hungry because even what you eat has little nutritional value! You can tell the difference when you shop at international stores. The vegetables, fruits and herbs smell stronger! No wonder immigrants prefer to shop at their own stores! This awareness led me to shop at international stores for oregano, particularly Latin American grocery stores. As an indigenous person from the Caribbean, I could tell right away that they were dealing with real oregano. The pungent smell was the first give away. The second give away was the taste. The taste of real oregano cannot be described unless like me, you grew up with it or in that culture.

Eating Swine

There are no errors in nature. The pig is a half-breed, created by a Black scientist to eat the filth of the Middle Ages. People in Europe did not bathe. They did not bury their dead. They suffered from the Bubonic Plague. The pig is a crossbreed between the aardvark, the rat and the dog. This creature had to be bred in order to clean up the filth that existed in that region. He was to be the ultimate scavenger. It is a scavenger no matter which way you look at him. The catfish is the scavenger of the fish family. (**Patient Heal Thyself**). Yet people eat it. Mind you, it has been prohibited. But the same people that profess to be Christian are the biggest hog eaters, and shellfish eaters. Either they do not read the Bible or do not care. Yet you find Muslims and Jews or Judeans following the proper dietary laws. Eating sea life with a shell lead to high cholesterol. My father never let us eat shellfish. These are scavengers and toxic beyond belief. These creatures were designed to clean up the heavy metals that accumulate in deep waters. Once you find out how toxic crabs, mollusks, are, you may think twice about eating it. **(How To Eat To Live,)**

We need to study biology, physics and other sciences a little closer so that we can understand what it is we are digesting. I want you to do better, so I tell you the truth. There is hope for humanity, if we would just act natural, live a natural lifestyle and refrain from eating that which has life. Life is in the blood. Flesh is so dense that it leaves itself in you.

Some people have been led to believe they cannot survive without animal flesh. Nothing could be further from the truth. There is plenty of protein in plants without having to resort to soy or animal life for protein. I will speak more on this later, in another section. But first I want to talk about how oxygen affects our health. Meat has zero oxygen. Any food that has zero oxygen does not belong in our belly.

Lack of Oxygen

Lack of oxygen will cause an unhealthy state in the body. What I mean by this is that certain foods produce oxygen and others don't. As you probably guessed vegetables produce oxygen. Chlorophyll produces oxygen. Cancer and tumors are brought about by a state of lack of oxygen. If you ever want to kill a cancerous tumor feed it parsley and see what happens. The tumor disappears due to the strength of chlorophyll in the parsley. That is an example of concentrated oxygen. The same is true for cilantro. You can buy cilantro just about anywhere now. It used to be that you could only find it in Latin and African stores.

Lemon is another super-food that has oxygen. Lemons and disease cannot co-exist. It is too alkaline for disease to thrive in it. Lemon has limonene and that is a good thing. Oxygen and cancer cannot co-exist. Microwave foods, most processed foods and canned foods have zero oxygen. Eat fresh.

Today's lifestyle requires "quick, fast in a hurry" attitude. For a long time, Malachi said do not use microwaves. Today the effects of micro waved food are being felt. How many micro waved dishes must we consume before our bodies cave in? It is a known fact that if you over-cook food it will kill the vitamins. Yet we over-fry foods with super strong heat in a machine called the microwave. That should be common sense. But we don't always show common sense do we? To use the excuse that grocery veggies and fruits are nutrition depleted engineered foods and then to resort to a carnivorous mentality is to pick and choose. That's like going to a bigger evil than to the lesser of the two evils.

Never do they think to buy organic or grow their own foods. If you cannot grow crops or shop organic, which is cheaper, then settle for the darn grocery fruits and veggies. You will feel better than if you ate meat and potatoes, which are heavy. We say heavy because we feel depleted after eating meat. And of course, this is related to the extra work required for the body to process meat. Did our creator really intended for us to feel tired after we eat? Most would say, "Of course not." That should be a hint to you. After I eat an avocado I feel refreshed and energized. Get in tune with your body. Notice how your body feels after you eat certain foods. Avocados have a lot of protein. But people also have a misconception about the amount of protein they should consume. Protein is also tied to body type, or should I say blood type. You should seek out books that address eating for your blood type. For my blood type, I am supposed to be a vegetarian.

Pollution

Bad air leads to disease state, though it can take years to develop. It is no secret that people's health conditions become better once they move to the mountains where the air is clean or any other such location. Once you become ill, you may not be able to detect it until years later. By the time a disease is discovered years of accumulation is already in your system. This is especially true of kidney trouble – the biggest silent killer of them all.

People who move to inner cities or urban settings struggle with respiratory problems. The following situations make the air dirty; vehicle emissions, chimney smoke, factory smoke, cigarette smoke, coal and grill burning, vapors from artists, aerosols, industrial activities, power plants, gasoline, airborne asbestos, waste burning, heating, plumbing, waste dumps, spraying buildings, spraying insect repellants near offices or by your house and the list appears to be endless. (**Cancer and Nutrition**)

Acid rain is now more common. When sulphur dioxide combines with nitrogen we get acid rain. Those two elements are very acidic. Sulphuric acid and nitric acid are the result of such a combination. This substance erodes such trees as fir, spruce, and birch. It also has a deadly effect on animal life and plant life. Acid rain is not just limited to the earth life. It also kills sea life such as fish and plankton. A metal such as aluminum can find its way from the soil into the sea. Aluminum is a very toxic metal and finds its way from the soil to the rain. After it rains you can find the following heavy metals in the water; cadmium, lead, and nickel. The water purification process is not perfect. Aluminum poisoning will eventually lead to renal failure. So for those of you who must see it in black and white you may look at **Cancer And Nutrition.**

You can find aluminum in deodorants. Whether solid or in spray form, the effect of aluminum is the same. The combination of spraying yourself with aluminum such as deodorant containing aluminum is self-inflicting. It is bad enough that this heavy metal finds its way into our air and water. Always read the label.

Cosmetics and Toiletries

Chemicals and aluminum find their way into beauty aids and toiletries. Anyone who uses deodorant, male or female must read the label. If it contains aluminum toss it out or don't buy it. I cannot say it enough. Aluminum will take your kidneys out. Yet the majority of deodorants carry it as part of the ingredients. Whether solid or in spray form, the effect is the same. I run a section of how to make your own toiletries in another publication.

Eating Processed Foods

We live a fast paced life, so we settle for the fast foods and processed foods. No wonder people are sicker than ever. Few people think to pack carrot sticks and celeries into their lunch boxes. We have strayed from the Mother Diet.

Heavy Metals & Pollution

People's kidneys get messed up for many different reasons. Some say heredity. But that too appears to be diet related. If your ancestors did not eat right they pass their flaws on to you. Other causes include, overeating, overdrinking, vaccinations, over the counter drugs, prescribed drugs, food choices, stress and more. Vaccinations are ridden with toxic chemicals, lead, arsenic, mercury, and cadmium, just to name a few. Our water system contains fluoride, and so do toothpaste. People buy into all this propaganda despite the numerous studies that prove otherwise. The rise in disease rate, plus people's own personal experiences, should be a clue. But due to miseducation, false lights, false weather, radioactive frequency bombardment by TV, microwaves and computers, coupled with subliminal messages built into the media, we buy into anything. We have been so dumbed down that we no longer question anything. In fact, we are drugged up more and more each day. The food and water supply contain drugs that damage the intellect. A whole book can be written on each item alone. You are being misled and have now become spiritual con artists, questioning the saints and the martyrs, praying only when in trouble; using biblical quotes at appropriate times [your convenience]. You also defend the system for fear of a missing paycheck. Never do you compare the prophet's movements and how their rebelling brought about mass change. Unless there is a movement towards the demand for environmental change, the Earth will become so polluted; you will not be able to come out of your house on certain days. All this is unnecessary. There exist a technology where cars do not pollute, but do they choose it? "Pollution, you know the truth, yet you choose, non-solution..." so goes my poem. Not everyone has an outlet. Some people settle into learned helplessness, which turns into apathy.

More On Vaccinations & Fluoride

Kidney disease can stem from chemicals, radioactive chemicals and heavy metals. I look at my amalgams and how I was forced to be vaccinated just to get into American schools. I see that the schools are not superior as they say. But most of all, I see reports about how vaccinations have not helped disease but rather increased it. I see that vaccinations put heavy metals in your system. You see people who still get measles and chicken pox who have been immunized. Many people dive their heads into the ostrich holes to escape reality thus ignoring the facts. You hear on the radio that vaccinations cause autism. **The Boston Globe Jul 2005**

Heavy metals are put in our water supply. Fluoride is put in our water supply. So is chlorine. Cadmium can find its way into our water supply. The fact that fluoride is a by-product of plant processing is nothing new. You can get fluoride from aluminum processing. Aluminum in deodorant is bad for you. Nor should you cook in aluminum pots. The records speak for themselves. Do your own research. Fluoride does not improve tooth enamel nor does it prevent tooth decay. Ask a dentist how to prevent cavities and he'll say use fluoride. I even had some tell me that it can be taken as a calcium supplement! This is what they teach in their so-called progressive schools. You either allow the blind to lead the blind; the wicked to lead the naive or you educate yourself.

For those of you who wonder how the kidney epidemic went from the thousands into the millions in less than a decade, remember what heavy metal poisoning does to the kidneys. Try to remember that humans weren't always vaccinated. There are many misconceptions about vaccinations. People somehow forget about studies after studies that link vaccination to autism. More proof that you are being dumbed down.

Pretty soon, you will be slaved with inserted chips.

The general public is being desensitized more and more every day. To use the excuse that computer chips keep track of missing children is a clever way to introduce the mark of the beast to unsuspecting people. A chip inserted in your hand or forehead will mean they will know where you are at all times. You have zero privacy. At this point you are not only an experiment, but also a robot! People are already slaves to corporate American when you think of the real price to make a living. Homes have skyrocketed for a reason. It is no coincidence that few can keep up with inflation. When you realize slavery is already re-instituted, then you'll believe. It is no coincidence that people who make up 13 percent of the population represent 50 percent of jail inmates. It is also no co-incidence that prisoners are currently picking cotton as we speak. They get eighteen cents an hour. Members of mainstream are suffering the crunch of the system. It is no coincidence that only one percent of the population control the resources. Vaccinations are now being imposed on older children, middle school and high school. Some face threat of being kicked out of school if they don't co-operate.

To begin with, you can't even attend school unless you get inoculated. If you keep your kids out of school you are truant or contributing to the truancy of a minor. The smart ones home school their children. Some mainstream people are being caught up in the system of the oppressors. Let him who hath an ear become more independent. The more you rely on the system, the sicker you become, physically and mentally. The spiritual con artist fools no one but himself. People used to be concerned with how many trees were chopped down, what animals homes were being taken. Indigenous people have always worked around nature versus against it. We are living in a society that is anti-life. The word antibiotics mean just that. Antibiotics are designed to kill bacteria, which are live. Problem is, it can kill you in the process. The same applies with chemotherapy. The cure can kill the patient. Natural antibiotic include Echinacea, oregano also meet the criteria. Heavy metal poisoning is serious matter.

Take colonics, get rid of your mercury implants or fillings, and take selenium and seaweed and or algae of every color. See the brown algae are for high blood pressure, whereas the green and blue, will address heavy metal poisoning. So don't make yucky faces at fishy tasting and smelling sea vegetables. Think of it as medicine. I am pretty sure you were probably made to taste worst than that. Remember cod liver oil and castor oil? Castor oil will rid the body of unwanted bulk in the intestines or stomach. It is a great laxative. Some now come in lemon flavor. For the less adventurous, you can simply place it on your stomach with a hot towel and it serves the same function.

The snake people that were here during the Adam and Eve story know. But they don't tell you about the collision and how this planet was changed out of its original place. Neither do they tell you about the multiple nuclear wars that have gone on without your knowledge. They don't tell you how they have tried to destroy us numerous times and how they plan to take over officially. They are already in power. Now they just have to make it official. The snake people show their skin. Do you have eczema, psoriasis, and webbed fingers, excessively dry skin? You probably have been mixed with the snake people. They walk and talk today just as they walked and talked to Eve. People get spooked out and fear takes over. They are so arrogant; they want to believe that in a vast universe that is endless, only one dot has life. How narrow minded. There are many suns out there. If the sun gives life and makes plants grow then why can't these same conditions be occurring elsewhere. The war in heaven was fought and it is now being fought here. One of the methods they use to destroy you is your diet. Other methods include vaccinations, medications, miseducation, media campaign, propaganda, genetic engineering and other modes. Your kids are taken away from you to be instructed in promiscuity - condom usage, false teachings about the food pyramid - to be carnivorous.

The list is endless; just as the battle of good and evil appear to be endless.

Mammals are not the only intelligent species. If you don't believe me, buy a cat and watch it carefully. Horses and whales are more in tune than you humans. They know to run for cover before storms hit. Elephants too. You used to be able to do this in times past. But you have been dumbed down. Your DNA has been manipulated. Oh and by the way, did you know food could change your DNA? What they put in food can change your DNA. And who are they? They are the agents. They are people who work for corporations who listen to the whisperings of the evil ones, the reptilians. I tell you what; since you don't believe me, do a research. Your topic should be "how certain chemicals in foods change your DNA" - just play with it until you find the truth. I really do not feel like sitting here lecturing to you so go ahead and do your own research. All I know is people, who eat healthy by the status quo standard, get sick anyway. That right there should wake you up.

All I know is I wanted to know why I got sick if I ate right according to what everyone around me was telling me. But what I found was more than I had bargained for. The more I dug, the uglier the truth became. This is why reading used to be prohibited. Yes, you guessed it. They want to control us as slaves just as before. They want to be worshipped just as before. Now they are trying to get rid of the Internet.

The powers that be put things in the air to destroy you. They fly airplanes in certain areas, leaving chemical trails. The chemical trails are a book unto itself. But even they admit chem.-trails are real. This is done to control the population. The most careful people can get caught off guard. Elijah Muhammad once reported that they admitted to trying to kill him by putting stuff in his water. They have the technology to put chemicals in the water in your home. A full house water filter would not be a bad idea. Whereas some report dry skin conditions, brittle hair and nails, the same people report the opposite when they obtain a home water filter.

Between what is put in the air, food, water, mandated vaccinations and who knows what else, you have your hands busy trying to undo the damage done.

We may not control the air, but we can control what we eat. Do not destroy yourself with what you eat. You already have enough going against you. One thing is television. You are being terrified into submission. The news is rampant with violent stories. What you don't know is the crime rate is lower than ever. But they manipulate the media so that journalists announce only the bad. They claim good stories don't sell. Let me ask you this - by who's standards – theirs? If you look at history they have always loved violence. The Romans and Greeks were entertained by violence through the Gladiators. There was human consumption by lions. Today, it is violent sports, football where hips are dislocated and spleens are punctured, hockey with metal sticks, boxing... Did I mention wrestling? How about wrestling bulls? The list is endless. What's with running from bulls to getting killed? Self-destruction is encouraged in every arena. Alcoholic beverage consumption is encouraged, and so is cigarette smoking. The TV used to be splattered with glorifying cigarettes in every movie, not to mention commercials. It's not until recently that someone put a stop to it. "Que sera sera" became a theme song on TV "whatever will be will be, the future is not ours to see." They want you to think you are not in control of your future.

The TV is being used as their tool for mind control. But you don't even see it. It is a lot of things you didn't see coming because you thought this was entertainment. Just as in Roman times, you thought getting killed in an arena was entertainment. You didn't see it as genocide. You didn't see that it was religious persecution. It totally went by you. If you want to play ostrich and not look at the violence perpetrated against humans, because it is too disturbing well guess what? Your head will be stuck in the ground when they enslave you physically with the chip under your skin. They may intimidate you. But that shows they have succeeded into turning the masses into sheeple.

Some people's intellect are being affected more so than others. It all depends on how strong your genes are and what your ancestors ate. How good is your memory? Do you remember anything prior to Kindergarten? That is my point exactly. Some don't remember Kindergarten while others remember being born and other lifetimes. What are you eating that is making you forget?

More Vaccinations

Vaccinations actually is a topic that should fall under the topic of heavy metals. It is filled with cadmium, lead, arsenic and mercury. In addition, it contains germs, pus and whatever other evils, strange minds concoct. It is believed that once you are exposed to something, you become immune to it. That may work in a certain respect such as you see when you travel overseas and strangers get sick but not the natives. But when you talk about injecting germs and heavy metals into someone's blood, there has to be an unknown consequence lurking around the corner. This type of experimentation has lead to the dimming of the cognitive abilities of children and adults. The link between autism and vaccinations is indisputable. Though today no child can enter school without it, there are alternatives. A person can choose to home-school, create their own schools or exercise their religious beliefs. But more importantly, one can use natural immunization techniques such as are employed by Dr Askari of Decatur, Georgia. Vaccinations interfere with your mission in life. Vaccinations force the kidneys to work harder. Remember, the kidneys are the body's filters.

Chemicals in Foods

Chemicals are used in food to preserve it and for appearance, as well as flavoring. Food has to remain on shelves longer than ever. People live further and further away from food growing places. Transporting foods from one place to another is another consideration. But the conveniences mentioned are hardly worth the dire consequence of dangerous chemicals in foods. There is no study to indicate what amounts of chemicals are harmful over a long period of usage. Food chemicals have proven to be carcinogenic. Nitrite is just one example. Since the kidney is a filter, the chemicals pass through the kidneys before excretion takes place. This causes unnecessary stress on the kidneys. Other chemicals in foods include cyclamate, saccharin, butylated hydroxytoluene and many others. For example, diethylpyrocarbonate creates urethan. (**Cancer and Nutrition**). The resulting compound led to health problems as well. Pesticides release chemicals into the blood stream of humans. It is not just direct spraying of vegetation. Animals that eat grass or vegetation get chemicals sucked into their skin and organs. These in turn wind up inside whoever eats the animals. Hazardous chemicals are so much around us that breast milk and infant placentas have been found to have toxic chemicals. Now you tell me, what is a brand new baby doing with toxic chemicals and heavy metals? Some of it could be traced to a mother's diet and the water she drank. Now let's get one thing clear here. We are talking about healthy individuals that were studied. These were people that were health conscious, suggesting that toxic soup is all around us. This reminds me of the poem I wrote called Sewer Sludge. The purpose of the poem was to bring awareness that some people have gone so far as to use sewer sludge as fertilizers. I also wrote The Miseducated Consumer in order to get people to read labels.

Agent Orange was found in babies. Have you heard enough yet? If you don't detoxify you will die. As much as you might hate the word toxin, detoxify and what have you, you will have to deal with it sooner or later. You probably are already affected. Now you must purify your blood after you detox. Then and only then can you even begin to address issues of concentrated neutraceudicals. Concentrated nutrition is only effective as a therapy when all the heavy metals and chemicals have been removed. Some chemicals appear in cleaning products that are commonly used in households. Some have innocent names like carbon tetrachloride. Others have scary names like formaldehyde. Formaldehyde is found in household cleaners, but it can also appear in foods. Ice cream, my people, has paint thinner. That's why in my poem called "What's For Breakfast?" I brought it up. People need to know these things. You also need to know that you can create agent orange by micro waving foods in plastic containers. It is also recommended that you do not use Styrofoam cups to heat things up in the microwave. The chemicals emitted in both instances are not pretty. People should not be using a microwave period.

Why not just eat organically? Save yourself a headache. No pun intended.

Alcohol

Alcohol consumption leads to kidney failure. Today's alcohol is more lethal than yesterday's alcohol. The alcohol of antiquity was meant as a tonic - to tonify the body and strengthen it. One of the ingredients was called strong back in a Jamaican tonic. It gives you plenty of energy and you need no food when you take this drink. It is fermented. Mauby is another fermented drink from the Caribbean Islands in general which was created to cleanse the body. Today's alcohol is designed to kill you. Okay maybe it was meant to relax you. I gave the benefit of the doubt. But think about it. Why would someone put chlorine in wine? Why put a harmful chemical called diethylpyrocarbonate in wine? This is a carcinogenic substance. This is why it is called substance abuse. The substances they put in recreational drugs and alcohol are designed to waste you away. You can say the same about tobacco. (**Good Health For African Americans**)

Tobbacco

Need I repeat it? Tobacco has formaldehyde arsenic, lead, cadmium mercury and who knows what else. Did I say formaldehyde? These substances decrease sperm count. Babies of women who smoke are likely to be deformed. Need I say more?

Pesticides

Neurological disease and hypertension and liver disease have been linked to pesticides {see Cancer and Nutrition}. How many potato chips do you have to eat before you develop health problems associated with hypertension? The same question is being asked of pesticides because there is an obvious link. We do not drop dead from it because of the small amounts in foods. But over time these chemicals, toxins and heavy metals linger on in your body. This includes pesticides and herbicides. Pesticides are changing DNA, number of limbs in amphibians, death of insects. Eco-systems are affected.

Cooked Food

You have heard that smoked food causes cancer. Well now there are new studies that prove that cooking foods can be hazardous to your health. Cooking takes away nutrients from foods. Since life is in the enzymes, you wind up eating dead stuff or denatured stuff. No wonder you are always hungry. Your body is craving vitamins, minerals and trace elements. The study also revealed that cooked food causes cancer. If you take a pet and feed it cooked foods such as we eat, and feed another one a raw diet, you will see a difference in their health. Eating cooked food is a personal choice. Many people have had good results eating raw foods.

If you are still cooking with aluminum pots, stop. Use stainless steel instead. It is the safest pot there is. As you learned earlier, aluminum poisoning leads to renal failure.

Foods And Politics

Judging from research conducted by Mr. Philpot of Grist.org, it seems the Feds are behind world hunger and the push for chemically laden foods. Sometimes farmers are paid not to grow food in order to create scarcity. This boggles logical minds. Every corporation has a franchise overseas, and the worst foods are being pushed overseas. So, considering that the Feds are behind every political move world leaders make, it doesn't surprise me that they have their hand in the diet either. Mr. Philpot points out the following. The government spends billions on corn products. Corn syrup is in many products. It is cheaper to buy junk food or products laden with fats and sugary corn syrup. Workingwomen are at risk of misfeeding their families because they have no time to prepare meals. The government is in their pocket, so what little they make goes to shelter and utilities. Chemically laden foods, high calorie foods and those filled with bad fats are pushed worldwide.

The feds responsibility in this is that they subsidized foods that create diabetes, especially in minorities such as African Americans and Mexicans. Interestingly, their diabetes shoot up, a diet based type of diabetes. Corporations find it more profitable to sell cheap foods. But cheap is not necessarily better when it comes to modern food. We pay less for these high calorie foods but pay for it with our health and waistline. Diabetes type II was at 41 percent between 1997 and 2004.

The obesity rate was reported to be higher amongst the poor, at 36 percent compared to the 29.2 percent for the rest of the population. So, diabetes disease is related to economics. And in my opinion, so is certain kidney disease. The fact that the feds subsidize certain bad for you food, while targeting Afro-Americans and Mexicans is reason enough to raise your eyebrows. Due to corn's huge payout, they encourage overproduction. Sadly, capitalism plays a negative role. Sometimes the tool itself is not bad, but it is how it is used. The same can be said for television. It is used as a tool to target the innocent young in particular. You see more commercials about snacks and high calorie foods than you do healthy foods. The deeper you search, the more dirt you find. People should wonder why hamburgers and chicken sandwiches are being sold for a dollar. If you drive around eloquent neighborhoods, you may notice that more fast food places are found in poor neighborhoods. That's just my opinion. One thing is for sure; wilted lettuce is more likely to be found in poor areas.

When it comes to food production, control, regulation and distribution, food politics plays a big role. According to the Global Banquet report, hunger does not result from scarcity. Hunger and scarcity are inventions by monopolizers. It is also pointed out that small countries do know how to feed themselves. The problem is politicians dictate who will buy what from whom and who will boycott whom. Think of market-driven chemically based foods and industrial agriculture picture emerges. Small farmers don't stand a chance. Sometimes they are paid not to produce certain crops. Sometimes good vegetables and grain are burned in order to create demand. The point here is that many different sources that have nothing to do with each other are reporting the same thing. The sources range from economists, farmers, agriculturalists, environmentalists, activists, sociologists and concerned citizens. In fact, security is linked to social development according to the film entitled Global Banquet. Would you believe that certain life forms are patented? You can get more information from animal rights groups, professors, church groups and university studies as well.

Caffeine

What do cola, tea and coffee have in common? Caffeine. If you have kidney problems, you are to stay away from coffee and chocolate. Coffee causes disease in the urinary tract. Coffee, like alcohol has chemicals that cause dehydration. Caffeine alters the DNA. One report says coffee is bad, the next says it is good. Did you ever stop to see who is writing these reports? Could some of them be lobbyists trying to promote their products? It does happen. Some say coffee speeds metabolism and make you evacuate. Perhaps that is true, but at what price? Why not use something else that is not as questionable? Most other countries use expresso size containers for coffee drinking. Americans have to have big cups. They super-size everything. When will they wake up and smell the coffee? Coffee abuse leads to low birth weight and mistakes in genes. For me, the mistakes in genes are enough to scare me. Goodbye coffee.

Coffee has also been linked to heart disease and breast lumps that are cancerous. Addictions are strong. People with addictions have unresolved issues. People simply need to decide if they will continue to keep getting whipped.

Coffee is one of those products that are surrounded by controversy. Some have linked it to strokes. Everyone with kidney problems is told to stay away from coffee. My skin began to improve once I stayed away from it.

Had we never strayed from the Mother Diet, we would not be in this predicament.

Chapter 4

Straying From The Mother Diet

Let's face it - we have all strayed. Some of us have strayed more than others. We eat coffee cakes. I thought I was doing something by eating lemon cakes. I told myself, it has limonene. Never mind the white flour. Boy was I wrong. It constipated me to the tilt! We succumb to the pressures of work and eat doughnuts and coffee. I convinced myself that coffee was waking me up. Some people drink socially as an outlet, or for various reasons. What with the preservatives, pollution, engineered foods, potato chips and vending foods. There's no telling just how polluted our bodies have become.

We used to eat plantains, yucca [pronounced "yooka"], cilantro, ginger, and many other foods considered of medicinal value, yet tasty. Avocados are such foods. I used to eat yucca. Once I found out how valuable this plant is I went back to eating it. The college years were "all you can eat" buffet-style. Other things I had stopped eating were plantain, coconut, and abichuela [beans], and legumes, which all happen to be rich in fiber. Now I read about how you should eat plantains if you have bladder problems. The price of straying from the mother diet! I felt silly swallowing a yucca pill. My brother kept telling me these people are trying to make money off of you. Now every fruit and vegetable is in a pill form. I remember my brother professing that in the future; there will be no food, just pills. That was in 1975. It sure has come true.

Some people claim to be sick of oatmeal and beans. To say you never want to eat these foods again is odd because they have so much fiber in them. The fact that they are cheap should be a plus, not a minus. Lack of fiber in the diet can lead to a compromised system. Other foods high in fiber in our repertoire were name (pronounced nyame), yautia, batata (boniato) and others. Our fast lifestyles lead us into eating fast foods in between taking the kids to little league, cheerleading practice and their part-time jobs. Hell, I strayed so far from my ancestors diet, I even ate shrimp. I had the nerve to taste catfish and crabs after years of self-discipline and being told not to. But not for long. The guilt was too much. It's as though my father were living inside me reprimanding me for eating that prohibited stuff. While he did not quote the Bible, he lived the diet in the Bible. Later, I found out he had a Judean last name. People on my mother's side did too. My venturing off to taste these prohibited items were a matter of wanting to see what the hoopla was all about. But the guilt was indescribable.

My Dad taught against eating shellfish. The Good book advocates it. I never understood why more people do not follow the dietary laws of the Bible. Whatever its source, it made sense. When you think how high in cholesterol shellfish is...when you think that these haram (prohibited) foods are scavengers designed to clean up the bottom of the ocean, then it makes sense. They clean debris and mercury, cadmium and other heavy metals from our oceans. The God of our forefathers knew what was best for us. The ancient peoples were extremely resourceful. They knew how to remove poisons from rooty tubers, plants, and certain fish. Whether they were taught by God, Extraterrestrials or ingenuity, the point is thy carried out the plans. What happened to us?

Whatever happened to survivor instincts? I'm not talking about survival of the fittest or individualistic thinking. I'm talking about collectively gathering for the common good. There is an emphasis on sugar, processed salt (poison) and other abnormalities that cause harm. For instance, the wine you see today is not the wine of yesteryear. Our peoples fermented foods and drinks for a purpose and it was done naturally, without the use chlorine as you see nowadays. No wonder our systems are compromised

Some corporations claim pork is cured. Fine, what is it being cured from? Worms you silly! And even the curing procedure has no guarantee to be free of tiny parasites that are too small to be seen by the naked eye. The same happens with water. So that nowadays most people have parasites, even people who don't eat pork. I used to tell my sister not to eat pork. One day the worms showed up in her freezer! She was so awe-struck she left it alone.

I was a vegetarian from birth. Many battles were fought in my mother's dining room concerning my refusal to eat meat. This had nothing to do with a call for attention as the other sister implied. This had everything to do with the fact that meat eating felt abnormal; the skin was tough, the meat was tough. It was hard to digest. I could tell how long it took to digest, because I was in touch with my body at that time. The college years "all-you-can-eat" buffet started me on the path of no return. Before that, I was Ms. Health Food store advocate. In fact, I got my other sister on the natural store buying path and now she got my Mom into it. My Mom's diabetes is kept in check because of this.

So the people are still puzzled as to why this would happen to me. Whether it was the mercury in my teeth, or stress, we may never know. Stress leads to indigestion. Indigestion leads to other problems. It aggravates situations. I always suspected it was stress. Today's lifestyle is unnatural. We trade hours for dollars in order to buy things that are normally free from the earth, such as air, gas, roof overhead etc. We are forced to hold our urine as we work in places like day care, teachers and toll free line workers. I fit all those bills. I worked all those jobs...to the day I had kidney issues and consequently, the stroke. Some will lead you to believe that it was much more minor than what it was. Then I met a man who confessed, he too had a mini-stroke which was a lot more serious than he led on. He said he had to fake being well in front of doctors and employers just to keep the job. I knew exactly what he was talking about because I did the same thing! But I would only fake so much. Physical therapy was imminent.

Another lesson I learned is, too much of a bad thing is no good for you. Some people will swear that our ancestors ate pork, catfish and soda all day and nothing happened to them. But I say they passed on bad genes to us as a result. Why are you suffering physically from birth? Why are younger people having heart attacks (age 13)? Don't sit here and tell me what we eat don't matter. Yes, our bodies are resilient. Yes, our bodies miraculously heal themselves. But how many potato chips does it take your body to notice something is wrong? How many bottles of beer does it take to throw it out of whack? Which straw will break the camel's back? My point is, too much of a bad thing is bad for you. And I have to agree that the quantity of foods we consume is killing us. I recall reading a book called "How To Eat To Live." It said to eat once a day.

I remember having battles with my mother over dinner. She was always trying to make me eat something I didn't want. I was a fruitarian from birth. I didn't even like salads, except avocados. But what got me was her insisting that without meat I could not possibly be healthy. You see, she was brainwashed by my aunt who moved to America and bought the protein myth. She also bought the milk and meat myth. She even bought commercialized toothpaste. All of this was foreign to us. Even at a young age, my common sense told me eating meat is unnatural. My sister thought it was a way for me to get attention. Little did she know, this was a real physical condition. Since I felt full most of the time, I was sure I was born with a small stomach. So after the inflamed kidney diagnosis, I asked my Mom about a kidney problem in our family history. She was baffled. My Mom kept asking me, are you sure they said "kidney?" I assured her.

So okay, I did not ease away from these bad things overnight. It was a gradual process. I enjoyed my mother's stews. What I was mostly protesting was the eating of meat. I did enjoy eating eating plantains, yucca, yautia, ahyuyama and other complex carbohydrates. I was never made aware of their nutritional richness and started listening to the pushers of the American diet. It wasn't until much later that I learned how potassium and phosphorus rich these foods are. You can boil them. Since they have their own tastes, they require no seasoning. You will find that the less you dress foods up, the more you enjoy individualistic tastes. What is astounding is how little time it takes to cook! Plantains do require olive oil and salt. Some people add garlic or onions, but it is not required. Some people add caraway to yucca and make a pie out of it with cheese. But these are the exceptions not the rule. They are simply variations. I am simply giving you these recipes so that you may see that you don't have to just pop pills. "Medicine" can literally be eaten. I also was unaware of the calcium content of these food items. They are, in fact, so superior to the potato when it comes to nutrient and fiber, that I wonder, why did I stray from the Mother Diet in the first place. Ignorance can kill. I simply did not know their nutritional value. Americans swear they are superior to every nation, and everyday, people believe these misconceptions. The ad campaign machine is powerful. People would do well to turn off the idiot box and think for themselves. Not all ad campaigns have your best interest in mind.

Coffee was replaced with chai gotten from gas stations. Lemon or pound cake for breakfast was replaced with carrot cake. But remember, I didn't start eating lemon cakes until my late 40's. Then I noticed the commercial chai was extremely sweet and made my teeth hurt. So I drank orange juice instead. At least it didn't have milk. Later the orange juice was too sweet and the Chinese doctor said stop drinking commercial orange juice. When you think about it, commercial orange juice looks nothing like squeezed fresh juice. I knew this being from the islands and all. I wonder what chemicals they use to preserve real fresh orange juice to make it look so orangy or concentrated?

Tea became my friend. But sugar went into tea. Even brown sugar or honey can be a bit too sweet. But I was addicted to sugar you see, by this time. It started out with me liking sweet fruits. Then I had been introduced to fudge. Parents and teachers should do better. Now they're giving sweets as incentives in school as some of us watch helplessly. Others have taken matters into their own hands by home-schooling their children.

Straying from the mother diet reminds me of the Biblical characters that strayed from the godly teachings and paid for it by losing their inheritance. They literally cut the length of years they lived by more than half. And we have cut that in half, so that now we live way less than one fourth of what Mother Nature intended. At the rate we're going, it's going to get worst. People are dying at age 40. Now compare that to 930. My aunt lived to be 120. Compared to Adam's 930 years that is a step down. Nevertheless Black people began to live as little as non-Black people because they have adopted foreign lifestyles, particularly eating habits and way of thinking. Before hospital were invented, what do you think people did? They used fruits vegetables, herbs and roots. Today even kids have heart problems. What are we doing to ourselves? You cannot help any cause in a bad state of health. You need to be around if you want to make a difference.

DYING TREE

WHAT DOES A DYING TREE LOOK LIKE?
THE LEAVES ARE WILTED
THE BRANCH MAY BE TILTED
JUST HOW A PERSON LOOKS WHEN THEY'RE TIRED
BENDING TILTING
LOOKING LIKE A WEIGHT NEEDS TO BE LIFTED

THE SKIN MAY BE DRIED
THE TREE MAY BE ARID
THE TREE WILL STOP GROWING
HUMAN HAIR STOPS GROWING
CAN A WILTED TREE'S FATE BE REVERSED?
WILL A TIRED PERSON'S CRIES BE HEARD?
PERHAPS A TIRED PERSON IS DYING TOO
DYING TREES OFFSPRINGS ARE DYING FRUITS

At some point I realized I was dying. It got worst later of course, but the trend was obvious. My hair stopped growing. My skin was dry. I had zero energy, no matter what I ate. I looked like a train had run over me. My eyes and face were puffy. The hair became gray. I had pimples - something I didn't even experience as a teenager. Being from the islands means I was beautiful. My teeth used to belong in a commercial. Columbus and Ponce De Leon swore they discovered the Fountain Of Youth in the islands. That's because due to the good diet [yucca, yautia, yame, fruits, vegetables, coconut, ginger avocados etc] people never age. I'm into my fifth decade and people do not believe my age, even though I look worst than ever before. To me, I now look like death. To them I look like a teenager. That's because they're so used to seeing so many fat undernourished people. When I go home, I cannot find any clothes that fit me. It is so embarrassing. That was when I was weighing 136 pounds. Do not laugh, because pounds equal bad health more times than not. Yes, I was the walking dead. A zombie. So now we see why the same size means different things in different countries. So that sometimes I wore a size ten, depending on which country made the clothes.

Chapter 5

Conventional Treatment

Once your kidney functions in the teens, such as nineteen percent kidney function, it is recommended that you go into dialysis. Dialysis is a way to filter the blood. It is clear that toxins have gotten into your body, along with heavy metals. This taxes the kidneys, which are a filtering system. Once your filters don't work, toxins stay in your body. This is dangerous because your body begins to feed off of toxins. Your body does not even recognize nutrients for what they are. Imagine throwing whole nutrients into a sewer. Do the nutrients remain whole or does the sewer trash contaminate the nutrients? A similar thing occurs in the body.

The following, are symptoms that I had; swollen face, ankles, weight gain, frequent urination, feeling of wanting to urinate but can't, lower back pain [not consistent], high blood pressure, smelly high yellow urine, bulging belly, indigestion, nausea. Other symptoms manifested later as predicted by the doctor. These were metallic taste in the mouth, and urine coming out sideways [not straight down]. These are latter stages and are considered dangerous.

I listened to my doctors at first, taking pharmaceuticals as prescribed. Then I began to have side effects. I will never know if the side effect from the kidney drug, induced the mini-stroke, or helped it along. Pollution, preservatives, stress, heavy metals and modern lifestyle affect our bodies in general. So "modern" is not necessarily better. When I noticed the side effects of headaches, joint pain and depression, I stopped. At this point I began to recall my love for natural products. I remembered taking slippery elm for urinary tract infection to stop the burning sensation. You can actually insert slippery elm in your vagina and stop a urinary tract infection dead on its track. As far as the pharmaceuticals, they worked but the burning would come back. You see, the symptoms were being treated. Conventional medicine is designed to camouflage the symptoms. It never gets rid of the root problem. I had replaced a bad habit with a questionable one. Commercialized chai addresses the caffeine issue, but it does not address the problem of sugar and milk. Once I realized this, I began to make homemade chai from ginger root, cinnamon (sticks/powder), cloves (whole/powder), and optional was cardamom pods. All these items are readily available.

If it's not in your kitchen, it's at the grocery store spice section or the health food store. But even better, you can always find them at international grocers, cheaper. They also have rare stuff like extract of cinnamon oil. I love using that for my teeth, which were beginning to rot at this point. Cinnamon, whether in powder or oil have an anti-microbial effect. Plaque just kept creeping out from my throat no matter how much I brushed. At this point I knew the problem was systemic. It had gone too far. Plus the urine was coming out sideways as the urologist correctly predicted. The good news about cinnamon is that it is good for the kidneys. It has anti-microbial properties. Cinnamon improves circulation and is great for stomach problems. Cloves are anti-fungal and work well with the kidneys. Ginger aids with digestion and is also good for circulation. These are fire foods/spices as some would say.

I was boasting of how I overcame kidney disease without the use of dialysis. You see by this time I had noticed several things. Billy had died of kidney disease. He relied totally on conventional medicine and ate as usual without changing his diet. Rhea, a co-worker was constantly on dialysis (four times a week, a big increase.) In fact she went into dialysis when her kidney functioned at a 20 percent functionality. I thought wow, mine functions only 5 percent and I'm not on dialysis just taking kitchen herbs! I also worked with Vickie, who was also a victim of kidney disease. I met her while drinking sandalwood syrup. She asked me why I was taking it. I told her for my kidney condition. I bought it at an ethnic store and she ordered one. Then gave it back to me saying her doctor said it was too sweet. Then I'm gonna die I replied, because I sure eat a lot of sweets. Aspiring vegetarians do this according to Sacred Woman author,

Queen Afua. In an effort to avoid meat, we go for sweets and white flour out of hunger. Vickie insisted that I not only watch my sugar intake, but that I go into dialysis because she feels much better afterwards. I explained that Rhea feels drained afterwards and how it's been scientifically proven that 90 percent of the people who go into treatment need four days off from work just to recuperate. I noticed Rhea sleeping in class right after her treatments. The Feds put up with her because she was officially on treatment that was recognized by them. So if I slept, it was not tolerated because I was not technically on dialysis. Vickie insisted that I get on dialysis just to avoid being harassed. Plus, she added, you could get disability. Why wouldn't I want disability, especially after all the ill treatment behind kidney dysfunction, mini-stroke masked behind a full-blown stroke, sexual harassment.

So I ask Vickie, what percentage were you when you went into dialysis? She said ten. "What percentage are you?" "Five percent," I replied. Her mouth dropped. From that day on she was real scared for me. "Are you okay?" She would ask everyday, do you feel dizzy? Go get your blood pressure taken, retire, go off on disability, even if you continue working like I do, they know I'm on disability that's why they don't give me a hard way to go." I still refused. Furthermore, I would make it clear to her I had no intention of going into dialysis. I told her that Billy died despite the treatment and Rhea is weaker and weaker in spite of dialysis and now people are collecting funds every other day to maintain her treatment. "These expensive procedures," I explained, "do not cure you. They kill you." She kind of agreed but said it's best to do both, conventional treatment as well as alternative treatment. I had agreed to do the alternative treatment. In my opinion it was the alternative treatment that was healing her not the dialysis. Her skin was clearing. But she was still pushing the dialysis thing.

The problem with dialysis goes further than I thought. Do you know you do not even need a license to do dialysis? No wonder the dialysis clinic in Atlanta insisted that I go on dialysis. They are in it for the money and couldn't even answer all my questions. They did not care to discuss alternative treatment. That kidney malfunction is irreversible is one of their beliefs. But I spoke to alternative doctors and they reinforced my belief that kidney malfunction is reversible. Don't get me wrong. I ran into some who were not sure. But that's how determined I was to find the cure. I kept on interviewing people until I found people who were as hopeful in their belief of the healing power of the human body as I.

I admit I did feel dizzy many a days and went down to the nurse. You see, home remedies in the kitchen can only take you so far. I had to do something more drastic. I modified meat intake and cut down on eggs. But most importantly, I took a colonics - three in fact. Doing a colonic is like having thirty evacuations [30 bowel movements]. I ate more raw foods per the Koyfman center's instructions. I should have known better; Malachi used to push raw foods. Even I was an advocate of that at once. Straying from good habits does not help.

When Neeta Black found out I was going to write a book about how I avoided dialysis, she said, part of the problem is super sizing everything. I have to agree that overeating adds to the problem [if not create it]. We have not only stepped into a super sizing society, but we encourage all you can eat venues. There are country buffets, Chinese buffets, and even KFC got in on the bandwagon. Some buffets have bland tasting food. But people go to them to stuff a hungry appetite or due to the fear of feast or famine syndrome. Coffee cups become larger at the gas stations and grocery stores. Yet the original size of a cup of coffee was the size of an espresso. In the Caribbean that is still the case. Some people swear that coffee causes the body to metabolize food faster. Whatever the case, I know it's not good for people with kidney dysfunction. It's bad enough that coffee goes hand in hand with sugar and milk, two killers. But then to encourage people to drink coffee all day long is a questionable practice. Offices do it. Coffee shops expect it.

Coffee shops should concentrate on add-ons like sandwiches in order to break the monotony. I cannot stop anyone from drinking coffee. I just know it does not agree with me. Maybe your body is different. Coffee is one of the most acidic products there is. That is the sole reason it is so frowned upon by kidney health advocates. One thing is for sure; people with acidosis need to stay away from acid foods. Good health reflects a PH balance that lien toward alkalinity. You heard before that disease couldn't exist in an alkaline state. So why don't we eat an overabundance of alkaline foods? What many people don't realize is that the people who started the coffee craze did so because they ate mostly vegetables, so that they were trying to balance their bodies out [or prevent diarrhea]. In America, there is no such thing as eating too many vegetables. America does not have half the vegetables that exist in Africa, the Caribbean, South America or the Orient.

Our own mouths are killing us. We over-eat out of boredom, or due to anxiety. Sometimes we eat to be sociable. Sometimes we eat because that is the American way. Whatever the case, we need to listen to the Master Teacher more. He said, "Sufficient unto the day is the evil thereof." That means if you eat more than you need, watch out, disease will come knocking at your door. Other countries like the Caribbean and Latin America eat only during certain timeframes. For example, no eating after 7 pm. Adamah recommends that we not eat during the elimination period. You can consult with her for details. Her telephone number is at the end of this in the appendix. Plant based food eating is ridiculed in my office. But when arteries get clogged from white flour products, people stop laughing. When the pork rinds create edema in their legs, they start asking me for help. What are you doing to keep your situation under control, they ask. We live in a society where people are encouraged to eat all day long. Corporations ensure that commercials serve as reminders for you to buy their products. But food additives keep us constipated. Some food additives include dyes, artificial flavors, monosodium glutamate, sugar, salt, corn starch, corn syrup, just to name a few. As food sits undigested, it collects toxins. In times past, people did not have to battle digesting dried non-dairy coffee creamer. Do you know what is the source of it? That is my point exactly. Most of that stuff is made in a laboratory.

The scariest part is that these chemicals in foods are there by design - to keep us dumb down. To keep us from questioning the madness, the rising cost of housing, the war overseas to steal resources and other questionable practices. They do not want you to think. You're not supposed to find out how great you are. Your goodness (godliness) is so profound, they marvel at how you are able to invent traffic lights and other inventions while being downtrodden. Wow, if you can accomplish that while being oppressed, imagine what you can accomplish if you are not? The suppression of the intellect has everything to do with the fact that they are trying to hide something from you. You are not supposed to become aware that you will be further enslaved. Far-fetched as it sounds, you are already enslaved. You just don't have any bars in front of you. But think about the fact that you have to pay for everything that used to be free, like water, land and more. With food additives that make you docile, you won't rebel. The last thing they want is another Nat Turner revolt.

We buy into overeating because all their institutions endorse it. You are told that you have to eat a certain amount of calories, per day to include a certain amount of animal protein, dairy, a certain amount of grains and such. What did people do before the RDA standards? Now you are being forced to read labels if you want to survive. Trouble is, most people don't know what they are reading. They feel they don't have time to look in a dictionary. Some of the words may not be in the dictionary. What do glycols and triglyceride do for you, I wonder.

We are not only trained into overeating, but these jerks are completely aware that overeating causes disease. If that was the case in the past, imagine now, with all the pesticides and herbicides. Not only have no tests been done to see what all these additives do to the body, but also they really don't care. All of this is by design. You are supposed to be confused, clogged up and constipated. The idea is you will be too sick to fight for your freedom, which is being stolen from you day by day.

Sometimes it is not just our own eating habits; sometimes it is our own mouths literally, as in the case of having amalgams. Back in the day, dentists would fill your mouth with mercury if you had a cavity. It is known that the Atlantean Empire fell in part due to lead poisoning in the pipes. The people went crazy due to lead poisoning. So, the question is, if this happened in the past, why would anyone want to repeat it? Lead and mercury poisoning cause abnormal cell reaction. The immune system no longer recognizes its own cell so it attacks it. Sounds familiar? Anxiety and depression ensues. Confusion sets in. Remember how they stole the crown from the queen? Confusion had already set in. {see my poem: How They Stole The Crown From The Queen}. It seems hard to believe that the past is repeating itself.

In the age of super-sizing, people are being fed more than ever. You find all you can eat buffet all over the place more than ever. This is something that is attractive for college students. But think of how your stomach is stretched. Think of the damage this does to your intestines. Who is likely to be healthier, a fat person or a skinny person? We know that everything is relative, but fat people, I would think have more toxins. Fat cells duplicate themselves. Cancer sets in this environment of toxicity and lack of oxygen. People who try to lose weight will stop eating. Self-starvation leads the body to store fat cells for emergency reasons. Fat people are more than likely to have high cholesterol than skinny people. We know there are exceptions to the rule. The only reason younger people have heart issues now are because of the toxic lifestyle we lead. But in general, overweight people tend to have greater health issues than slim people. If you are fat, for example, you are more in danger of having diabetes or heart problems than a skinny person.

I was put on conventional medicine for kidney and high blood pressure. However, I began to have side effects. Not that this should be a surprise. My doctor even warned me about the side effects. The difference between others and I is that I was not willing to put up with the side effects. I felt as if I were going to die. When I go, I want to go as naturally as possible. I thought to myself, "it is time to explore alternatives." I began to research. I resorted back to the original diet eventually. One of the people at the organic farm that we were a part of once said, "if it doesn't grow on a tree and fit in the palm of your hand, don't eat it." How right she was. I had brought a lot of people into the organic farm. I was even editor of Organic Times and did a radio show on the topic. We had yoga classes, and rode horses. It was nine miles from Atlanta, but more than fifty miles from me. As I flashed back to the organic farm days, I wondered why did we stray so far from our original lifestyle. We fed a lot of people. It was the same way with my mother. She grew up in a farm. During harvest time all the farmers would share crops so that everyone would eat. There was no compulsion and that was the beauty of it. No one forced anyone to participate. It was voluntary and everyone was at peace. My

Mom remembers the days when her and her brothers would make perfume by crushing flowers with rocks. I remember days when I would enjoy the beauty of rainbow colored flowers all around me. Now, where we are at, you're lucky if you can find two varieties. Beautifying your surroundings really soothes the soul. That's why I engage in art.

I had a bad reaction to the conventional medicine. I was becoming sluggish. It was making me drag my words. My neck was hurting. I felt death knocking at my door. My conventional treatment was leading to a dead end of dialysis. I spoke to the person at the dialysis clinic and I came to one conclusion. They want your money at any cost. Not surprisingly, they do not encourage the alternative treatments I was talking about as an option. The sad news is no good reason was given other than that "conventional doctors know what they're talking about." She seemed inexperienced in alternative treatments. I often find myself having to explain to nurses and doctors how I treated myself naturally. They seem to want to hog this information, demanding answers, only to turn around and invent a new medicine out of the herb. Why do we indigenous people so freely give? We seem to understand that all was created by the all for all. The most precious life-giving elements are free - air, water, earth and the sun. We can heal with all four.

One nephrologist promised me he would not refer me to dialysis and that he could cure me alternatively. I got really excited. He hugged me and promised to take good care of me. When I got a call from the clinic, the person could not verify the use of alternative treatments. I asked if they use conventional medicine and she confirmed. After I interviewed her thoroughly, I realized they were a clinic that existed solely to test new medicines. "We see how these medicines work with your body, and we change them if we need to." That right there tells me we are just their guinea pigs. Don't get me wrong; maybe it will work for some people. I am just not willing to take the chance. I kept looking for alternative cures. Someone knows something, they're just not telling it. That doctor probably saw dollar signs in me. He promised me alternative cures, yet the secretary swore they use only conventional medicine. I came to the conclusion that a drug company holds the fort. You have to be a researcher like me if you want to cure. And don't settle for the first answer from people who are trying to pay their medical school bill.

I believe that some doctors keep you sick so they can profit. They usually give you the most expensive medicine first. When you think about it, how would they profit if you were sick? It is not in their best interest for you to be well. The sooner you realize this, the sooner you can begin to stop depending on conventional doctors for your healing. No one is taking away from their ability to deal with trauma. I am saying they get their medicines from herbs and roots to begin with. So why don't you go directly to mother nature? Once Mother Nature products are tampered with, they do not work the same. This is what Dr Llaila Afrika explained in his book. There are micronutrients not yet understood by scientists that work in conjunction with vitamins, minerals and enzymes. For instance, there are phytochemical... and other micronutrients involved.

People go to stores to buy vitamins separately. The best bet is to eat the real thing - fruits and vegetables. But if your area is short on this particular vitamin or mineral, then by all means take a supplement. If you must take a supplement, go to a health food store and read the label. Watch out for fillers, such as cornstarch, wheat, eggs, you name it. Yes, you even have to read the label at a health food store. It's your health. Guard it with your life. A good supplement is MSM with green algae because it's all natural. Mix it in juice, so you won't have to deal with after taste. I take the one called Renew Me, which I buy from the co-op/health food store.

Buy honey with the honeycomb still in it, so you can disguise the flavor of things. If you are not able to use sweeteners regardless of source, then develop a taste for things that are good for you. You may also use apple juice to disguise the flavor of many things, including vegetable juice such as celery juice. Dates and figs also hide bad flavors. It seems strange that the most beneficial remedies are free or cheap. The sun is free, yet its health benefits have not even begun to be explored other than that it provides vitamin D. If you are in tune with your body and nature in general, you would notice how much better you feel when under direct sunlight. People who have the flu or a cold suddenly breathe better when they get up and are exposed to sunlight. Sunlight is also the only substance that gets rid of mold. The science of the sun was known in ancient times. People mistakenly believe they were involved in sun worship. But the reality is these ancient Afrikans and melanated people of the West knew the science of the sun. When I write, I go to the deck, so that my body can benefit from the sun's rays. I love the sun. When I go back home, I sometimes don't eat. But the energy from the sun keeps me going. It renews me. Have you ever noticed that you do not need as much food in the summertime as the wintertime? In the winter we eat the sun in the form of chlorophyll from the vegetables.

As I sat in front of my computer at work feeling drained, I wondered how many other people feel as I do. How many people see the correlation between computer usage and feeling drained? How many people associate fatigue with television watching? And I'm not talking about messages that make you psychologically depressed. I'm talking about electronic waves that zap you off energy. You feel it as you turn on your radio in your car. If you are in tune with your body, you notice these frequencies of energy. On the contrary there are people that are so drugged up by food, water and vaccinations, that they don't see any further than their next paycheck.

Someone pointed out to me how obvious it is that the general public is being over-drugged. They use the plavix commercials as an example. Never before have we been bombarded with so many anti-depressant commercials. you create your own alternative. Even over-the-counter drugs were created with an ulterior motive. Deep inside you, you know the love of money is the root of all evil. Deep inside you, you know we are no longer living in a spiritual world. Children are being drugged in the schools, despite the findings about Ritalin and Prozac. Even recently, they admit teenagers are more violent than ever. These drugs have been connected to violence.

But we ignore the obvious statistics and allow ourselves to be lied to. You fell for the lie about fluoride in your toothpaste. You did not read the medical journals, and scientific studies. Their own evidence reveals that fluoride has nothing to do with preventing cavities. Their studies reveal that fluoride is a by-product of the aluminum companies. The studies show it to be not only a waste product but also a product that dims the intellect. No wonder you have fallen for so much crap! The 10% brain usage has now been further reduced. Your critical thinking faculties have been tampered with! It's in the water you drink, the shower you take, and the food you cook with. And every time you eat out, you ingest it. Thinkers buy their own bottled water and water filters for home usage. Thinkers are problem solvers. You, the general population are too busy defending them, exactly what you were trained to do. Thinkers don't even call you people. They call you sheeple. And their favorite saying is "sheep get slaughtered."

Formaldehyde gets put in cigarettes. Ice cream has paint thinner. Some items meant to be ingested for human consumption has rat poison. And so do some medicines. When are you going to wake up and do research? Do you smell the coffee yet? Even healthy people get sick under this system! You even think inserted chips in your skin are cool because your children won't get lost, and you won't have to worry about getting robbed. Yet the good Book tells you it is the number of a man, 666 is the mark of the beast. The beast is this whole out of control system and you accept the devils mark every day. Your license has a chip in it. Your credit card now has a chip in it. You are being trained to accept computer chips in your plastics, so that when they announce everyone must accept it in their skin, it won't seem so bizarre. No one shall buy or sell anything, except those that do not accept the mark. It is a conscious choice. You can accept to be drugged up or not. Why would you take something that you don't know what's in it, or how it is made? I tell you what, you go on taking rat poison and all the other stuff, but when you get sick, don't say I didn't warn you.

I will now share my poem with you, called "Health Consciousness"

HEALTH CONSCIOUSNESS

THE REVOLUTION BEGINS AT HOME
A CULTURAL HEALTH CONSCIOUSNESS
MODERN CHOICES TAKE A TOLL
ON OUR PRECIOUS HEALTH.
DE-NATURED, DE-VITALIZED FOODS
LEAD TO WEALTH
FOR OPPORTUNISTS - NOT YOU

WE'RE TEASED WITH OUTWARD BEAUTY
PRETTY CAKES, MEAT COLORING
JUICE ADDITIVES
VEGETABLE WAXING
IT'S REALLY TAXING
ON OUR HEALTH.
LET'S TAKE A STAND
LET'S LIVE OFF THE LAND
FAST FOODS AT WHAT PRICE?
IS YOUR SOUL THE ULTIMATE SACRIFICE
WHEN WILL YOU SAY SUFFICE
CHILDREN BEING POISONED WITH VACCINATION
SLOW HOMICIDE, SUGAR, DENATURED WHEAT
ADD RITALIN TO THE HYPERACTIVE EQUATION
AND DEATH ENSUES
TAKING PILLS AS HOSPITAL BILLS
KEEP PILING
THE CON LOBBYISTS CONTINUE SMILING
MAKING DEALS WITH THE NEW DRUG PUSHERS
PHYSICIANS

My friend whose father is a physician agrees with me. She loves her Dad dearly. But let's face it - Doctors have been trained to push drugs for pharmaceutical companies. Look at any doctor's journal and who do you see advertising? You guessed it. Drug companies. The side effects I was having from the kidney medicine, the stroke medicine, the sexual battery medicine all had side effects. I was dying quicker from the side effects than anything else. At some point, I made a decision to get off legal drugs period. It was at a time when I was moving in slow motion. What I have learned is that natural medicine leaves you with zero side effects and more energy.

The President of The Gambia was discredited for finding the cure for aids through a dream by his ancestors. Yet the founder of the Mormon Church found the church based on a dream. Constantine was also shown a dream that he should conquer through the cross. He saw a sign of the Cross in the sky and thus accepted Christism, which he turned into Christianity. The double standard is when you accept norms for some and not others. The pattern is clear. For example, doctor Sebi went to jail for claiming to cure aids. Need I say more? It becomes clear that the people that run things are not interested in cures. I got real sick and am now using myself as an example of what not to do. Do not become a starch eater to avoid meat. Just eat vegetables. Find a way to make them taste good. Use sauces made from natural thickeners such as arrowroot, not white flour.

It's a shame that people cannot share their healing modalities without being questioneded. Anything outside the convention is looked upon as superstition. But the very people doing the ridiculing hold the biggest superstitious belief. It really wasn't that long ago that bloodletting was taking place. Not to mention using leeches to draw out bad blood. Rather than taking out blood they should have been cleaning it. Detoxification does just that. Today they have moved up one notch by using dialysis. Dialysis is an attempt to eliminate bad blood or toxic blood or rather replacing it. But it leaves a lot to be desired. People report being exhausted for the next four days. They move about like zombies as they are zapped off their energy levels. Is this long recuperating period really necessary or is there a better way? The answer is yes; there is a better way. Do you know that you do not have to have a license to do dialysis? Enough said. The powers that be want you to believe that kidney disease is irreversible. They want you to believe that once your kidney malfunctions it can never go back to its original state. When kidneys go back to their normal function you do not hear of it from the medical profession. Nor do they speak about spontaneous remission from cancer. Why should they want you to be well? They were forced to pay big bucks for their education. Not all doctors are wicked. I do admire their ability to deal with trauma and other issues of health. But I am concerned with the numerous diseases contracted in hospitals. I am concerned with deformities brought about by their own drugs. I am concerned about the diseases caused by vaccinations. I am concerned about the side effects of conventional drugs whether over the counter or prescribed. We rely too much on people who not too long ago came out of caves, practiced bloodletting and used leeches to treat medical conditions. I in no way put down all doctors because I know everyone is different. One thing I know is that the trainers of doctors are not inclined to teach about using nutrition to heal. You will hardly hear them telling you to saturate your body with minerals in order to heal. You will not hear them talking about

Echinacea, garlic, St John's Wort, bucchu, or burdock. They will not tell you to eat parsley or celery. Yet all these things help various conditions and kidney function in particular. They will not tell you that real salt does not cause hypertension. They will not tell you that table salt is a poison. They will not tell you that sugar is a poison. They will not tell you that sugar is processed with pig's blood or that Doritos have pork in them. They will not tell you to go on a raw food diet in order to let your body heal. They will not tell you about the elimination period and how you should not eat at that time. They will not tell you what time to stop eating or what time the digestive system goes to a halt. They will lead you to believe that aging is normal and that aging begins at forty. Yet the patriarchs lived much longer than a century. They will not tell you to eat one meal a day like Elijah Muhammad did and how that lengthens your life. They allow you to eat all day, all night and do not educate you. Your healing is not their concern, but making a profit of the pharmaceuticals is. Rather than recommending more vegetables, more fruits, they give you a pill. Did you know that plants could heal every disease known to man? Whether that plant is called a vegetable, a fruit, a root or an herb it still heals you. Did you know that green mature lechosa could heal certain kidney conditions? You may wonder why anyone can benefit from green papayas or green plantains. But that is because you are not familiar with its chemical analysis. When you study the chemical analysis of things then you'll understand why Fo-ti and her shou wu chi cure the same ills. You will also understand why food grade hydrogen peroxide is a cure all and why DMSO cures the same thing. It all boils down to having similar chemical analysis.

The medical establishment may be aware of some cures and not others. The key is of those they do know about, why aren't they teaching it? The medical professionals are made to take the Hippocratic oath. I think it is hypocritical that they take the Hippocratic oath but teach the opposite of what he taught. They're not democrats, they are hipocrats (smile). Hippocrates taught that food is medicine and the relationship of astrology and wellness.

Your best bet is to talk to alternative doctors who have studied these sciences. I am speaking to the skeptics right now so bear with me. Another thing you may want to try is research on the Internet certain free articles on the subject. Keep an open mind.

Think of how others healed prior to conventional medicine and "practicing" physicians. I have nothing against doctors. But if they look way older than me and are younger, and if they die early of the very things they are treating, how much do they know? Why did my aunt live to be 120? Why are my other two aunts ninety-five and walking briskly wherever they go, with their senses intact? They weren't forced to take vaccinations or amalgams and their diet was intact. They also didn't bathe in chemicals.

That's another interesting observation. Why is it that Alzheimer does not exist in some countries? Why does it only exist in modern industrialized countries? Think about it. At some point you will have to admit that the primitive life isn't so primitive after all. They ate raw more than they cooked. They ate organically [free of pesticides and herbicides]. They knew the science of removing poison from certain barks and tubers. They knew to detox from food by using castor oil. How much credit are we giving our ancestors? Give credit where it's due. I look older than my brothers and sisters because I have had a much tougher life, yet, with all I have been through; I still look very young for my age. People tell me all the time, so this is not bragging. My point is that by utilizing something as simply as the healing power of foods, herbs and water, we can do much to improve our health. We can use water as colonics/hydrotherapy; infuse elements found in plants, draw heat to create natural saunas and so much more. We can use our hands to massage, or our fingers to pressure point. We can even use our thoughts, in well wishing as we direct intense love for those who need it.

We are so careful that we read labels. There is nothing fanatical about that. Nowadays they put swine in everything. Certain glycerin derives from pork. Even Doritos and Cheetos have pork. This is as recently as April 25, 2007. By their own words will this continue, unless enough people write to them. You know how it is. Many things are the way they are by popular demand.

Our forefathers ate organically, raw and they did not overcook things, nor did they use microwave. You can bet that the water was not filled with chemicals or radioactive heavy metals. You have to ask yourself why if they know this stuff is harmful do they put it in our food, water and environment? Could it be population control? Deliberate genocide? Money making tactics?

All of the above? Whatever the reason, one thing is for sure; you will have to change your lifestyle if you want to survive.

Now why don't they teach survivor skills in school? These are the thoughts that you need to replace your old ones with. For as soon as I replaced old way of thinking with the expectation of receiving, that's when things started happening. Stay away from negatrons. And pray for those who are lost. The more people you help, the more you help yourself.

We should not feel that we are limited in how we heal. Sometimes combining Western medicine with eastern medicine is a good idea. You can analyze someone's health by studying their blood. If you are so inclined, some alternative health clinics employ both conventional and alternative treatments and analysis combined. To the other extreme are those that employ only alternative analysis, such as determining disease through hair samples, which is equally valid. There are many ways to obtain the same goal. I tend towards the latter for the following reasons.

Mistakes in Dialysis

As time went by, I found out that there are many errors committed when it comes to dialysis. Mistakes are not publicized much because it causes lawsuits and raises insurance costs. Dialysis is simply a temporary solution. It is not a cure. Your blood is filtered while you wait for a kidney transplant. That's it. It is not even intended to treat the condition. Once you commit to dialysis you are on a one-way street. Very few people get kidneys. There aren't enough people donating kidneys. Then you have to be on medicine for the rest of your life if you do find a match. The reason for this is that your body treats this new kidney as a foreign object. Your body knows that it is not part of your body.

Rather than face such dire consequences, simply replace old habits with better ones. Cure yourself. Explore alternative treatments. When you do what I am telling you to do and you heal, do not go back to your old ways. Replace old habits with better ones.

Chapter 6

Replacing Old Habits With Better Ones

HERBS

You may be thinking that kitchen herbs are just that, but you would be surprised at their other uses. Why do you think the Spice War took place? Why do you think Magellan sailed around the world? His trip came about as a result of the demand for cloves and other spices. Cloves came to Spain by way of him in 1512. Prior to that Black people were using it as anesthesia, for indigestion, hernia, respiratory problems, nausea, parasites, toothache, sterility, for fungus and bacteria. Today you find it in commercial products like Lavoris. You can use it in liquid form as oil or as powder or whole cloves. As oil, it is very strong. Please do not use the oil in large quantities or undiluted. I use very little for gum problems. I make a tea out of the cloves whole or the powder. If you have toxic problems they can surface, showing up in your mouth.

Herbs are inexpensive and they do work. The Chinese give you commercialized "tea" said the founder of CKLS/New Body Products, "A tea whose health benefits are questionable," he continued, "yet they only drink sage." That stuck with me. I stopped drinking commercial tea with the exception of herbal tea. Other than that I do it the way my folks have always done it - use the real thing. I recall my Mom never bought commercial tea. We drank oregano tea when we got sick, along with cloves tea and ginger tea. If you caught a cold she would put a lot of garlic on the food - all with a third grade education. Some people cringe when they hear of oregano tea, making a yuckie face. I don't have time to beg people. Either you want the information or you don't. As it turns out, the oregano you find being sold commercially is depleted or grown in bad soil. But being from the Caribbean I recognized the real thing when I saw it, smelled it and used it. I bought mine from the Mexican stores. The tea is powerful. No wonder we healed as children when we were given this powerful good tasting tea. It brings back to me good memories of my loving mother showing that she cares. Oregano oil can be used as an antibiotic. The strange thing is, that commercial antibiotics don't work. Oil of oregano has been proven to work where commercial antibiotics fail. In other works, people have not been successful at replacing Mother Nature. You can get oregano oil at health food stores for twenty dollars. If you simply want to make tea, it costs two dollars for a lot, at a Mexican grocer. Either way you take it, you are looking at anti-fungal properties, along with, antibacterial, and anti-viral properties. It is even considered an antiseptic, which means, you can use it as a mouthwash, provided you dilute it. As to why people ignore the nutritional values of oregano is beyond me. It is probably for the same reasons they ignore the nutritional properties of yucca. They see the word and think, yuk. Simply, put, they did not grow up with the Afro centric or islander culture or "Ladino/Latino culture. Melanated peoples knew that oregano has calcium, boron, manganese, A, C, potassium and copper.

There's more, but who has time to list it? Oregano has phenols and carvacrol. These are potent substances that lab folks use for medicines and some of the properties are just now being discovered. Meanwhile, you stay in the dark while making yucky faces. What this means in layman's terms is that oregano has worm expellant properties. My Mom taught me to never eat meat unless I cooked it with oregano. She said all meat can be seasoned with oregano and oregano makes everything taste good. All Americans [meat-eaters] have parasites and most don't know it. If you are constantly hungry, that is a sign that you have parasites. If you have bad breath and a coated tongue, you could improve it with oregano by creating a gargle solution. If you have kidney problems, you probably are displaying a wide range of symptoms. Once the digestive system is affected, the symptoms are too wide to name. But they all can be helped with oil of oregano. The good news is, oil of oregano can be used both internally and externally. I sometimes rub my stomach with it. Oregano spice can normalize blood pressure. Oregano kills every possible virus there is. It has been used as tea since time untold. People show surprise when they see me making oregano tea. All they can think is, "isn't that what they put on pizza?" But they never think to ask where the pizza people got it.

Alternative Treatments

Back to Earth - Clay

People always have me buying them health food items or natural beauty products. Like the clay I am so dedicated to. I use the internal red clay for detoxification, and the external one for skin eruptions. I never had much skin eruption as a teenager because my diet had been pristine. Now I see that eruptions are a result of a toxic system. We are dust. We are clay. The elements in clay are in us. Clay brings the body back to balance. It has a magnetic field that pulls toxins out of your body.

Replace Meat or Use Transitional Foods

Meat in our culture is used in fewer amounts than in America. I have a Caribbean background. Most cultures on both sides of the continent eat less meat than Americans. They also live longer. The ones that die usually die of preventable causes like lack of technology to purify water. At the Koyfman Center in Norcross, Georgia, I learned that it takes the body four hours to digest meat. It really made me think about curtailing my meat intake. Funny, my significant other used to battle with me in an attempt to make me eat meat. I was even encouraged to get fat if I ever wanted to get married. The pressure to be fat lead me to binge eating at the college buffets. What a mistake. I have never been the same. And now these same people call me fat. At some point I was using tofu, soy burgers, soy hot dogs and soy bacon. These are transitional foods for people who are not ready to go cold turkey. Looking back now I would have gone cold turkey sooner. I think of how none of these transitional foods have fiber. This makes it hard to digest. You must flush everything out with fiber or you are challenging your digestive tract. Fruits, vegetables, figs, dates and coconut have fiber.

Replacing Coffee with Chai

I replaced coffee with chai. Coffee made me feel drained. My Chinese doctor and regular doctor said stay away from coffee. Chai has ginger, cinnamon, cloves, cardamom and black tea. The problem is I was buying commercialized chai instead of making it myself. So the chai had milk in it and this upset my stomach. They also add too much sugar to it, so it tends to irritate my stomach as well. Eventually I began ordering the chai from Barnes and Nobles because you have the option of having a soy-based chai. If you make your own tea, you need to watch that sugar or else you are defeating the purpose of the infusion.

Eventually I had to replace bananas. I ate them for the potassium content, but since I had a weight problem they had to be dropped. Some people are laughing right now. They don't think I was ever fat. I was weighing 136. That was too much for a 5'1 person. Wait till you hear how I lost weight. Fatness to me was relative. Everyone in my family is slim and I had curves, so what is fat in one country is slim in another by definition. I have a hard time finding clothes in my country at 136 pounds.

Specific Teas that Cleanse & Address Circulation Problems

Cloves became one of my favorite teas. Cloves act as an anti-bacterial and anti-microbial agent. Cinnamon helps with stomach problems, sugar glucose balancing and circulation. Lord knows I had poor circulation. Cinnamon is also an antiseptic. Cayenne and ginger help with circulation as well. My circulation got so bad; I could barely drive without my right foot hurting like hell. Sometimes I felt the pressure on the arms and fingertips, as if blood just wasn't reaching it.

This is dangerous. Many diabetics have had their limbs cut off due to circulation problems. Something tells me this can be avoided. Try exercising, standing on your head, or lifting your body in a yoga position upwards as I instinctively used to do all my life. This was before I even knew yoga existed. Isn't it interesting how our bodies talk to us? When I was younger, I was so in touch with my body. I knew right away what I was allergic to...chocolate, peanuts and tomatoes. It simply made my tummy ache. Today, we are so caught up in the rat race, we don't know which way is up or down. But one thing is for sure. Many people with kidney problems become diabetic.

Other teas that are helpful are lemon tea and anise tea. Anise helps with digestion, nausea and with water detention. The chemical anetol in anise is what aids with digestion of food. During the time of the Pharaohs, anise was used for the aforesaid reasons. Others use it for hiccups and even cancer. Both men and women can benefit from anise. The men get hormones that help with the prostate, while the women get milk for their babies. Studies have shown that anise help rebuild cells in the liver. The better the liver works, the better the kidneys work. Lemon has so many benefits; I don't know where to begin.

Originally I would eat a healthy breakfast, compared to my latter years. At the beginning of course we were all exposed to the usual bacon, eggs and toast. I wrote a poem about this called "What's For Breakfast." What it boils down to is you are eating dead embryo, white flour and pork! We would also eat plantains, yucca etc. The egg, bacon thing started after coming to America. In my later years I was so caught up in the 9-5 grind that I would grab a lemon cake or an egg sandwich. If you ever want to know how to get the kidney to dysfunction just inject yourself with egg whites. That's all you had to tell me to get me to stop eating eggs. It was going against my culture to have a sandwich period. We are "slim" because sandwiches are not part of our culture. I replaced the lemon cake with carrot cake. But, it is still white flour. Then eventually I had to give it up altogether, because after all, it is still white flour. It made more sense to eat yucca with garlic for breakfast. When you think about it, it takes no time to boil yucca. Ginger tea or cloves tea should replace coffee. Think about it, the most acidic foods are combined into one drink; coffee, milk and sugar. Our Mom used to give us the following teas whenever we got sick; cloves or ginger or oregano. One at a time. There was no combining or mixing of foods in a crazy way. Beets were regular part of diet. Fresh beets have a distinctive taste. You feel the live enzymes. I later found out that beets detoxify. Now if you take it to another level, you'll drop all man-made vegetables. Some of the vegetables that you see today are not part of original Mother Nature. They are man-made. Beets and carrots, though great at fighting certain diseases are not original vegetables. Do what it takes to get you healthy the most natural way possible. Eating organic is certainly the way to go. Even original foods like oranges are being tampered with through genetic engineering. {Poem, Genetic Engineering speaks on this subject.} Anyone who has a kidney disease should consider detoxification. The kidney is the filtering system in the body. Once the kidney go out or dysfunctions, you can literally become toxic in more ways than one. You will face toxicity from food laying undigested as well as heavy metal poisoning. That is the world that we are currently living in. Chemicals are in the water, the air, and fresh foods in the form of pesticides. The best route is to go organic. Aren't you worth it? You need to start thinking about saving your life.

Just as sure as the doctors predicted, I began tasting metal in my mouth. The urine also began coming out sideways. That's a bad sign. When I saw all these symptoms coming to be, just as the doctor had predicted, I began to get more serious about getting out of the kidney predicament.

At some point I do recall replacing meat with texturized vegetable protein/soy products. The soy hot dogs, soy bacon, soy hamburgers and soy sausages all tasted like the real thing. You just had to know which brand to get. My favorite was Morning Star. Still, I recall the products making me feel full quickly. How long did it take to digest these products, I wondered. Little did I know I was sacrificing fiber in the process of trying to eat healthy. The lesson you can learn from this is that no matter what you substitute for what, always include a healthy dose of fiber in your diet. In other words, keep the vegetables coming.

Natural Laxatives

I recall taking CKLS and how no other product would work as efficiently as that one. CKLS stands for colon, kidney, liver and spleen. It contains aloe vera resin, chamomille, chaparral, red cayenne/capsicum, cascara sagrada, mullein, uva ursi, fenugreek and dandelion. Uva ursi and dandelion are diuretics. Aloe vera attacks the parasites due to its bitterness. "But this is too simple," I protested. It's too cheap! At that time I thought that for a product to be effective, it couldn't be cheap.

Now I was being faced with paying expensive prices for the same ingredients...aloe, hydrangea, chamomile and bucchu senna combinations. Each ingredient plays a role in this kidney dysfunction problem. Slippery elm and tea tree oil address the itchy burning sensation. If you take slippery elm internally, it will help with digestive problems. Slippery Elm is soothing and nutritive. For this reason it is recommended for ulcers. Tea tree oil is also anti-bacterial. Bucchu is a diuretic. Cloves are anti-microbial. I drink it more frequently now. Take notes. Cheap is sometimes good for you. Kitchen herbs heal. No house should ever be without the following herbs and roots; cloves, ginger, oregano, cinnamon and garlic. After sugar gets the best of you, you will need cloves in liquid form for that toothache. Cloves will also address that pile you got in your belly putrefying. Ginger will help digest the indigestible when your system gets lazy. If you have kidney issues, you usually have a potbelly. Oregano is more miraculous than people give it credit for. In my culture it is normal to make oregano tea. If you could feel it's healing power you'll see why. Now they're tooting it as a miracle breakthrough. And of course, they're charging an arm and a leg. I just laugh and go to the local international stores. Talk about pennies on the dollar.

Purify Your Blood

As a person with kidney dysfunction you need to think about purifying your blood. When you go into dialysis that is exactly what they are trying to do! (Purify your blood). So if you could purify your blood without feeling totally drained and unable to work, would you try certain herbs and or infusions or root foods? I took sorrel to purify my blood. The blood purifiers I took were burdock, sorrel, Echinacea and a lot of garlic. Beets also purify the blood. Garlic was a favorite. Garlic reduces cholesterol, fights high blood pressure, and clears the arteries from plaque. It also reduces ulcers and tumors. Think about the tumors that form from piles of food and tumors love sugar. I would use it on my navel in liquid form because I learned that what goes in the navel goes to every part of the body automatically. There is a hole on the navel from the time you are born when your cord is cut. I also used liquid garlic in my ears. By this time my ears were affected with tinnitis. Tinnitis can come to toll free users, but of course the Feds would never admit to that. I inserted tea tree oil in my ears upon the insistence of a melaleucca seller. Prior to that I had gone back to using lemons as purifiers because no disease can exist in the presence of lemons. Wish I had kept it as my favorite from infancy. The price for straying from the Mother Diet. Unfortunately, I was so much a part of the system that my own treatments were done in spurts. Still they were so effective that I was still left standing while others were dying around me from kidney dysfunction. Vickie could not believe that I was still standing a year later, let alone two. She just couldn't fathom it. A combination of alternative methods and prayers were at work. I told God I was not ready to go because I had not yet accomplished my mission. I almost died several times. My pet (cat) saved me several times, licking me after I passed till I came to. My energy returned after that. I was aware I received a healing.

Another method I used to purify my blood was through wheat grass. Eating wheat grass is like receiving a blood transfusion. That says it all. Your alkaline level rises. I personally chew it and spit out the indigestible portion, since I don't have a juicer. That works fine for me. The taste is slightly sweet, to my surprise. My cat loves it. Have you ever noticed that animals gravitate to green things when they are sick? I spent fifteen dollars at a time on wheat grass, determined to do a "blood transfusion." But you can spend as little as two dollars at the local coop or health food store. My cat won't eat it once it starts going bad. Once it loses its smell it has little nutritional value. Cats seem to have more sense than humans. Many of us think that health food stores are more expensive than regular stores. I say it depends on what you get and what it does. Co-ops overall are cheaper than regular health food stores. So are their organic foods.

During purification I would take alfalfa because of its nutritive value. Alfalfa has vitamin K, E, D, C, potassium, magnesium and calcium. Since it reduces cholesterol it became extremely useful during the mini-stroke convalescing period.

Becoming A Vegetarian

Have you considered becoming a vegetarian? You smell better internally and thus externally. All the deodorant in the world does not hide the stench from rotting animal flesh (you have eaten) inside you. Leave a piece of meat out for several days and see what happens. These same parasites thrive inside you. What makes you think you're special? Your body is warm, and this is the environment they thrive on. Have you noticed that the biggest animals are vegetarians? When it comes to people, also, the more vegetables one eats, the healthier one tends to be. The exception is those who develop a sweet tooth. That's when they start eating pies and cakes. But in the meantime, there are plenty of super-green supplements. Many of these supplements have anti-oxidants, green algae and grasses. Otherwise you can just purchase vegetables. The advantages of the grasses and algaes is that they get rid of heavy metals. This means you don't have to go through the chelating process, if you cannot afford it. Just know that all people with kidney problems are dealing with heavy metal intoxication, along with food intoxication. A vegetarian has a wide range of choices. There are green vegetables such as zucchini, lima beans, string beans, kale, cilantro, parsley, cabbage, and broccoli. Let's not forget avocados. Then there are the purple vegetables, such as purple cabbage, purple lettuce, grapes, berries and so on. The yellow vegetables include squash, carrots, sweet potatoes and so on.

The Protein Myth

As soon as I was told that too much protein caused the kidney problem, I suspected meat was the source of that bad protein. I stated my hypothesis right upfront. After my book was finished and some insisted on eating meat I find out that I was right. A well-known doctor announced that animal fats and flesh are responsible for kidney dysfunction. Please read Cancer and Nutrition. Although my mind was already made up based on my research, I include this source for those of you who need a little more convincing. I am happy now that I see that there are so many studies that corroborate my hypothesis. I have been saying this for years. But bad habits are difficult to break. I cannot expect people to change overnight. Habits become addictions. Although, there have been people who leave meat alone overnight. Again, I will not judge. Bone marrow is supposed to reverse kidney function, not the meat. We used to eat stew with bones, and we would eat the marrow. My mother said bone marrow is good for you.

Many people think they cannot survive without animal protein. What you don't need is animal protein. You can get bad cholesterol from animals but not from plants. What is not advertised is that many other foods in nature contain protein. Avocados and hemp seeds have plenty of proteins, to name a few. Some plant-based foods have proteins but in proportion to what the body needs. Other foods have plenty of proteins such as beans, legumes such as lentils, seeds, such as pumpkin and nuts. I mentioned hemp seed because it is so high in protein. Did you know that ginger has protein? Just about every vegetable has protein. Nature has created a balance. Do not buy into the animal protein lie. In fact, animals have less protein than other natural foodstuff. People should just eat for their body type. Some people were created to be vegetarians. You can tell this by the teeth structure. For example, ever notice teeth that are so straight, small and even? These are your natural born vegetarians. You might even detect the length of time a person lives, is a telling factor concerning health. The following cultures live longer than Americans; Japanese, Latin Americans, West Indians, people from Tibet, and many others. Usually the people enjoy fresh air, sunshine, and an abundance of plant foods as intended by nature. They usually eat little if any processed foods. If they die young it's usually because they have moved to an industrialized country and adopted their habits. Ironically, though the U.S. has a great hospital system and boasts great improvements in sanitation, other cultures outlive them. And if they do die young, it's usually because of some sanitation issue such as water contamination. This is not to say the people are "backwards" as some would have you think. It's been proven that water purification systems are purposely kept from "third world" peoples. Environmental racism is a problem that has not come to the forefront yet. But it does exist, and many people will come to my rescue on this. Environmental racism is when government or private services fail to be distributed evenly across the board. To be more specific: it is when sanitation services fail to pick up trash in ethnic neighborhoods, to make them look trifling and filthy. Then the populace begins to play the game called blame the victim for the crime. Now let's talk about how I overcame the economic game of trying to afford expensive treatments for life-threatening situations.

Protein is pushed because some people have a love affair with meat. But now that you know how meat eating started, it should repel. Even more disturbing is how it is processed. But it gets worst. The toxins and parasites it produces in you will take quite a while to reverse. Some people are so out of touch with their bodies, that they do not see the correlation between their illness and meat eating. Many are clueless as to how they got high cholesterol. Some wonder why they have such a hard time digesting food. Still others do not see the connection of pimples and being carnivorous. Doc used to say that's the worms or parasites coming out. Then you have those that wonder why they have a body odor.

Letting Your Digestive System Rest

People simply don't let their digestive system rest. Before food such as meat finishes digesting, which takes four hours to digest, people are putting more food in their mouths. So the intestines never rest. This is just too much burden on the digestive system. And we wonder why we are sick. If you consider the pounds of sugar and meat we put in our system it is staggering. It is truckloads in quantity. And we wonder why we are sick. You simply have to ask yourself, was the body intended to take this type of abuse? Did the Indians Black or Red have any intentions of polluting us with sugar when it came to chocolate [the food of the gods] or was sugar added after colonialism by the Europeans who enslaved them and forced them to produce sugar cane? Black's health began to improve when they consumed the sugar cane in its natural state. But the health deteriorated when it was forced upon them as processed. This says a lot. Processed food is simply not good for you. If this is by design, the devil is laughing at you right now. If not, then you are foolish to fall for somebody's ignorance. The sheeple have been so dumbed down, that the average person thinks the color of sugar is white. I have literally heard someone say this. The sad part is, once it is processed, it is robbed off its nutrients. This brings to mind, table salt. Real salt is pink, whereas real sugar is dark brown. By the way, the brown sugar you buy in the grocery store is not natural either. That's white sugar with molasses. Real sugar can be purchased in Latin American stores, and the syrup can be purchased in some Arab stores. The good news is once you purchase these items you discover a good taste. Tea tastes better and it doesn't make your stomach hurt. The minerals in these foods are abundant. Why anyone would remove minerals from a product is questionable. What is their motive? Whatever it is, you want to run real fast in the opposite direction when they start giving advice.

Aspirin Substitutes / Anti-Inflamation Substitutes

As aspirin substitutes, I would use white oak bark, and cherry bark. Boswella also has anti-inflammatory properties equal to aspirin. The good news is that it will not irritate your stomach like aspirin. Black raspberry and yucca are also good for pain. Pine resin has proven to reduce pain also. You can get it from your local co-op.

Would you like to see what intestines look like for meat-eaters versus vegetarians? Would you like to see dirty colon versus a clean colon? Doctors can tell you the story. They get to see it everyday when they do operations. They can tell you what organs look like before they kill the host. Some of us don't want to know. We close our eyes like the ostrich sticks her neck in the ground in the face of danger. For some of you, it could take a picture to convince you to stop that lifestyle. For others, it would take you getting sick to finally jolt you into reality. For others, like me, it could take a near death experience. I never expected this to happen to me considering how I found meat to be so abhorrent as a young child. Lifestyles can be addictive if everyone around you is doing things one way. After a while you begin to feel like an odd ball, sticking out like a sore thumb. But now that I know the difference, being an odd ball makes sense.

You may not smoke. But if you are around people who smoke you may be exposing yourself to unnecessary chemicals, thus increasing your toxicity. Cigarette smokers leave trails of formaldehyde, cyanide, nicotine, lead and whatever else the cigarette industry decides to poison you with. My car key fell under my car. I crawl under my car, only to inhale chemicals from a cigarette butt, that someone had left at the library.

Mercury Fillings Replacement

I haven't had extra money to remove my mercury fillings yet. But people show a difference of toxicity when they remove their mercury fillings. After all, mercury is a heavy metal. Some people claim health benefits immediately after removing their mercury fillings. Others don't think it's worth the trouble because of complications in removing the mercury. In other words, the mercury may be too far into the gums, so get a dentist that know what he/she is doing. That's a judgment call. Just remember, mercury is a heavy metal, no matter how practitioners may try to disguise it. The same is true for fluoride.

Changing Your Water Supply

Fluoridated water is not all that it's cracked up to be. Fluoride is placed in toothpaste. Yet the fact remains that it is a heavy metal that harms you. But, you don't have to take my word for it. There are countless studies on the subject. Now why do you think people push fluoride? As it turns out, fluoride is a byproduct or waste from processing plants. Yes, they were trying to make a buck at your expense.

It is better to use distilled water than spring water. Distilled water has zero contaminants. You will have to supplement yourself with natural minerals. Be careful never to supplement yourself with anything created in a lab being passed off as natural. Attend health food expos whenever you can, so that you can compare. You may do just getting a water filter. Some filters gather gook, then you eventually drink gook if you don't change it every so often. The best thing to do is to use the Wellness filter. It not only filters water in a superior way, but it provides natural minerals because of the natural rock sift it goes through while implementing a superior technology.

I don't expect everyone to suddenly drop all their old habits and replace them with new ones over-night. Although, there are people who have done this. One person that a nutritional counselor spoke to did just that. Everyone is not like him. Some people need transitional foods until they adjust to a whole new lifestyle. As long as people understand that these are transitional foods and that there is something better, that is all that matters.

I shared the following poem with a co-worker friend. She died laughing. We had a good laugh about it. I wrote it at a time when I was sick and tired of being sick and looking for an alternative food-style.

WHAT'S FOR BREAKFAST?

IT'S SATURDAY NIGHT AND YOU THINK
NO MORE RAT RACE OR CLOCK PUNCHING
AND JUST AS YOU BEGIN TO SLEEP
THE ALARM CLOCK GOES BEEP BEEP
IT'S SUNDAY MORNING
WARNING! WARNING!
THE DAY IS NOT YOUR OWN
SOON YOU REALIZE YOU'RE PERFORMING
ALL THE CHORES ALL ALONE
COOKING...LAUNDRY...SHOPPING
COACHING...TAXI-DRIVING
LEGITIMATE STUFF
YOUR KIDS GO "WHERE ARE MY SOCKS?"

YOUR SPOUSE SAYS, HONEY
"WHAT'S FOR BREAKFAST?"
YOU SAY, "BACON, EGGS, AND TOAST"
"LET'S SEE; DEAD EMBROYO, WHITE FLOUR AND PORK!"

HE SAYS, "WHAT'S FOR LUNCH?"
YOU SAY "MEAT, LET'S SEE; PRESERVATIVES AND
CYANIDE
HE SAYS, "WHAT'S FOR DESERT?"
YOU SAY, "ICE-CREAM, LET'S SEE; PAINT THINNER"
HE GOES, "WHAT'S FOR DINNER?"
YOU GO, "JUST LIKE LUNCH, MEAT;
PUS, BLOOD AND INSECTICIDE!"

Now keep in mind that nowadays, there are also multiple ways to analyze someone's condition. You can analyze the tongue, hands, feet, eyes, using biofeedback. Hair analysis reveals the status of your health. The aura can be analyzed using Kirlian photography. Certain machines reveal brain wave patterns similar to a cardiogram. The idea is the same but less invasive. There are some people who are on fixed income and cannot afford expensive machines. But keep in mind that just as there are fancy machines in expensive neighborhoods that can analyze what is wrong with you or keep track of your progress, there are also more economical ways to get to the same goal. You can employ the services of local whole food pharmacists. In Georgia, there is Doctor Chris of Snellville, in Brooklyn, there is Queen Afua. Look through magazines such as Natural Awakenings or Aquarius and you can begin to compare prices and services. There is something for everyone. The same way they put concentrated nutrients using an IV, they can study one drop of blood and tell you a lot about yourself. So it does depend on where you go as far as affordability is concerned. So shop, shop, shop and compare just as you would with a conventional doctor

Chapter 7

Inexpensive Remedies

CKLS, DMO, Hydrogen Peroxide (food grade)

Like most of us, I become suspicious if something is too cheap. Our natural reaction is "it must not be any good." The same is true for furniture. But in the case of herbs such as are combined in CKLS and it's potency, the owner of the company probably believes in making it affordable to people. You can obtain it at Sevananda for $18.00 in Atlanta, Georgia. You can also get it for $11.00 as a distributor. The energy supplement called concenergy by E. Excell costs the same if you are a distributor. Do not believe every report you see. Food Grade Hydrogen Peroxide costs $11.00 at health food store on Beaver Ruin Rd in Norcross, GA. Life's Essential sells it for $14.00. DMO is another miracle cure-all. The same can be found at the Beaver Ruin Health food store called Nutrition Depot. They each treat so many diseases yet are so cheap. The two latter products provide oxygen to the body. The same can be said of EON water.

A Black man invented the recipe for kidney, spleen and liver disorder into a product called CKLS. This product contains fenugreek and dandelion, aloe vera resin and cascara sagrada. Well lo and behold, these same products are found in expensive remedies.

I also recall telling Don about the organic Farm in Loganville GA. I was a part of that move, bringing people left and right to the farm. You could save a lot by participating in the co-op. What a wonderful way to save on fruits and vegetables. Here I learned that one should eat only what can fit in the palm of the hand. I also learned that sugar is the enemy. The inventor of CKLS [New Body Products] also talks about the damage sugar can cause.

Cheap Ways to Detoxify

Dr. Sebi tried to tell us about cheap products that cure aids. Instead they tried to put him in jail. So we know who is behind that - the people who have financial interest, of course. Again, I found that no one product eliminates the problem because there are several problems going on simultaneously. That's why you cannot take a magic pill. I had to address blood purification issues and toxic chemical issues. Dialysis is designed to address both. But so is selenium and algae, except that they don't have the dangerous side effects.

Earlier I had researched how one female got rid of her high blood pressure without taking pharmaceuticals. She took brown algae. I took, brown, green, blue and red, because they each address a different symptom and I was experiencing all the above. My advanced kidney condition came with several prices. I had high blood pressure so I took brown algae for it and also bitters from Africa, Sweden and the Caribbean (Trinidad and Jamaica}. I took blue and green algae for heavy metal poisoning removal. Whether the heavy metals came from metal implants (fillings made of mercury) or whether it came from eating tuna fish everyday in college, or crab salad or fish period, is not clear. The important thing is that we have enough chemicals to contend with so why add fuel to the fire?

Finally, you can get heavy metals out of your system by using glutathione. A health food store clerk told me about this. These natural pills cause the brain to produce a substance that gets rid of heavy metals. It's cheaper than doing chelating therapy. Most healthcare providers want to do a $250 analysis just to figure out what's wrong with you. Others charge from $900 to $8,000. So if they both get you to the same goal which way would you rather go?

After going through all the procedures so far mentioned, the bio-analysis tests showed no signs of kidney problems for me. I went for a second opinion and got the same results.

Drink More Water

One very inexpensive remedy for people with kidney problems and urinary track infections is drinking more water. We are made of 70 percent water. The brain sits on water! Babies wade in water before they are born. In nature, there is more water than solid. The Earth itself has more water than land. Blood is made up of elements found in the ocean. Fruits have more water than pulp or seeds. Papayas, watermelon, peaches, oranges and mangos all have plenty of water. Coconut fruit is full of water. We drink coconut water during fasting. You can survive in an island drinking nothing but coconut water. People who do not drink water develop kidney problems. So it is logical, that if you have kidney problems, you need to increase your water intake. The kidneys utilize gallons of water a day to filter toxins out of your body. I had a dream where the elders were criticizing me for not drinking enough water. They showed me what hydrated organs look like versus mine, which was dehydrated. Mind you, this is just before my kidney problem was even discovered under X-rays.

One reason I did not like drinking water is because of the way it tastes. Come to find out, it is the chemicals they put in water that I find so offensive. They give water that metallic taste. Toilet water, sewer water and other waters are purified with bleach to make it drinkable. Fluoride and other heavy metals are added, so don't be surprised to find cadmium or lead in your water. One sad reality is that the people that purify the water are not at all sure how much is too much bleach or chloride. They even admit that they are guessing! Ladies and gentlemen, we are their guinea pigs. A lot of information is kept on the low-low. I started out drinking spring water to counteract this. Some people say tap water is being sold as spring water. I was later told that distilled water is best for kidney sufferers because distillation gets rid of the chemicals and heavy metals. As a mater of fact it is recommended that you take the detoxifying clay with distilled water. Later I also started taking ozonated water because it hydrates you at the cellular level. It really does make me feel better, especially the one produced by the EON Beverage Group, Inc. This is free advertising for them but go to www.essenceoflife.com. Better still, go to any health food store and they have it at prices comparable to spring water. For what it does, it is so worth it. Talk about controlling your kidney function! So I buy it by the case. Always saving a buck. Furthermore, it encourages me to drink more water. We must keep in mind that our bodies are made up of 70 percent water. Not only that but tap water will take you out of this world. Because of all the chemicals added to tap water in an effort to purify it, the water becomes a health concern. You in turn suffer with kidney dysfunction. Remember, the kidneys filter all liquids and purify the blood. The kidneys become taxed when too many chemicals are involved. Never before in the history of humanity have we ever been exposed to so many chemicals and heavy metals! You feel hydrated as soon as you drink this water. It even regulates body temperature while assisting the kidneys to eliminate toxins quicker.

Take Natural Diuretics

People with kidney problems get kidney disease for different reasons. It could be stress, heredity, eating habits or a different disease that affects the kidneys, such as obstruction or high blood pressure. But sometimes it could work the reverse. High blood pressure may not necessarily precede kidney disease. Sometimes it is vice versa. However you get it, the symptoms may or may not be similar. Here are some symptoms that kidney sufferers display. High blood pressure, frequent urination, inability to urinate, edema/water retention, inflammation, indigestion, poor circulation, bladder infection and I'm sure you can think of some other ones.

Since we are talking about urinary problems right now, let us talk about an herb that addresses that issue. The herb that is beneficial to people with urinary problems is horsetail. It is a diuretic. It is amazing that this one herb deals with issues of edema while serving as a urinary remedy. On top of that, it is also great for kidney function and bladder health. There's more. Horsetail alleviates kidney stones, renal infection and infection of the gallbladder. I have a suspicion that gallbladder infection and kidney problems have a common root problem. Anyway, if you take horsetail as prescribed, you will not be visiting the restroom at night. But you need to use it under the supervision of an herbologist. It has a minimum amount of gold in it, which is good for arthritis. You may make an infusion or use it as a tincture. Remember, all these herbs can be found at your local co-op of natural products. Horsetail has selenium. Selenium does addresses issues of toxicity, but the amount are to be determined by a professional since opinions vary.

Other diuretics include celery, celery seeds, parsley, watermelon, bucchu, and uva ursi. When you drink little water, the body begins retaining water as if to prepare for a drought or desert like conditions such as a camel faces. I had great results with these, especially watermelon.

The Indians of both North America and South America (to include the Caribbean) used dandelion as a diuretic. This diuretic keeps blood pressure in check, helps with digestion and liver problems.

Dandelion is one of my favorite diuretics. It has proven to help increase the flow of urine and reduce swollen feet. This is not a bad way to control blood pressure. You may even hear that you can lose weight with it. One thing is for sure. It is great on salads. It is also known for having vitamin A and C. Of course, if you talk to American Indians, they'll add more benefits as well. For example, they might say it helps with diabetes because it regulates sugar. My thing now is, if it's green, let it in. Just don't rely on diuretics for long periods or as a weight loss mechanism. You should at least replace the potassium level when you use diuretics.

If you decide to fast for cleansing purposes, coconut water is an excellent water replacement. It has the same electrolytes, as Gatorade except it is natural. You can buy these by the case in the Latin stores or any oriental store.

Other Natural Laxatives

Have you noticed that people with kidney problems usually have a protruding belly? That's because once the kidney is compromised, one no longer digest food. The body becomes so toxic; the food just sits there, especially if you are not eating fiber rich foods. In some cases, fiber rich foods are not enough to ward off the toxic soup of chemicals. The same was true in my case. Thus I had to resort to laxatives at first. The problem with laxatives is they make you dependent for digestion purposes. Commercial laxatives are in particularly dangerous because of this. One of the best laxatives is CKLS, which contains Cascara Sagrada and aloe resin, which is bitter. Anything bitter usually makes you go. I learned this from the Africans.

Another alternative is for you to use figs and dates, which are both rich in fiber. Boy, do they work! Try to buy them as fresh as possible. You would be surprised to find out just how soft they are when fresh. Try the international grocers. Coconut has an incredible amount of fiber. Apple and apple skin is another sure way to make your undigested food pass. Eating mango skin is another way to force the digestive system to work. Most foods that improve skin like mangos and papayas, will improve digestion. Mango's fiber content can be seen with the visible eye. Pineapples get the gastric juices going. Cucumbers also get the gastric juices going. You can eat them raw or juice them. It has been said that string beans get the gastric juices going but I didn't eat enough of them. I never liked string beans. I put up with it.

I use flax powder because it behaves similar to psyllium husks. In addition, it contains the good omega oil so sought after. If you buy it ground you can make natural bars with it, combined with your favorite bar recipes. I combine with pineapple powder, dates, alfalfa and oat. In another section I speak of cod liver oil and castor oil. I tell how these now come in lemon flavor. You may also wrap a cloth around your stomach, which as been soaked in castor oil. It will be as though you literally ingested castor oil. You can find one such cloth or package at a health food store. I would just use a hot towel. There are no rules. Only the ones you make. The limit to your healing depends on your imagination.

Eat a Variety of Vegetables

Where I work, I am exposed to computers all day and people eat all day long at the vending machine to counteract the negative conversations with huffy clients. Did I mention snacking keeps you awake? In reality, eating dead food [not raw] puts you to sleep. But we have been trained to believe "food" such as potato chips keep us awake. You'll be up long enough to keep from bumping your head, but it is no picnic. When you have a cold, how do you feel after you eat salty dried snacks? So why ingest it period? Why not just eat things that make you feel healthy all the time like soups, fruits and vegetables?

It's bad enough being surrounded by vending machines that sell junk food. What is sold in the cafeteria is no better, because it's all fried food for the most part, combined with dairy products. I would hit the salad bar, when I would visit the cafeteria. But the salad bar is limited, so eventually that gets old. What I should have been doing all along was bringing my own lunch or salad. Vegetarians have it good because there are so many vegetables to choose from. For those not familiar with this reality, just visit any real farmer's market, especially the international ones. You can also visit any international grocer. Our lives are enriched with variety. Meat and potato is boring. To every potato, we have seven similar such product.

Addressing Food Toxicity

Inexpensive remedies cannot be taken for granted. They always work and I always go back to them. But sometimes the dysfunction is so systemic that we have to take drastic measures, expensive measures such as colonics, expensive herb combination, and detoxifiers. Do not be afraid to spend money on your health. It should be the most important thing because without it, you are nothing. All the money in the world will do you no good unless you have health to enjoy it. But more importantly, you need to be concerned with helping people - your people - who are at a loss. So if you have not accomplished your mission, I suggest you concentrate on bettering your health. A sick body is not of use to the Lord. Why defile his body temple in the first place? A sin against you is a sin against nations. It is mass genocide. Every sperm killed, every egg that dies represents wasted potential. Stop the Madness! I had to hold my horses and stop the madness. What was the point in healing if I was going to turn around and poison myself again? What was the point in doing colonics if I was going to fill the emptiness with hard to digest meat, sugar and white flower? Therefore, cleanse yourselves and sin no more. It makes sense. Some remedies that I find helpful from the health food stores are uva ursi, bucchu, and sorrel. Actually, I get sorrel from the Jamaican stores. It soothes the stomach. I use the root, but I hear that the leaves purify the blood. Adamah recommends I use bladder wrack mixed with Irish moss for nutrition. Bladder wrack and kidney troubles go hand in hand as the name implies. It detoxifies the bladder.

For my teeth, I use cinnamon oil or powder. As you know, when you are infected, it can show up as plaque or halitosis. Cinnamon has astringent qualities. It not only has a sweet taste, but it expels gas and is great for the kidneys. Celery seeds have a diuretic effect, so I make a tea out of them. They are a bit salty. But this is natural salt, unlike table salt, which the cells have no use for. You may just try to eat the celery if you don't like the taste. If something hurts me bad enough, I develop a taste for it. Speaking of developing a taste for something; some people think you have to develop a taste for avocados. Avocados already have a taste. If you buy Haas avocados from regular grocery stores, you may find, some are tasteless. That's because you do not know how to pick an avocado. It cannot be too hard or too soft. Buy any brand except Haas. If Haas is all you have ever tasted you are seriously missing the real thing. Go to African, Latin or Caribbean stores. The skin must give, just a little. Furthermore, you may find delicious ones if you buy them from the organic section or the health food store. You may even try an international farmer's market. The problem with the regular grocery stores is they readily accept engineered foods. Have you noticed that fruits don't taste the way they used to? They either taste like dirt or watered down. If you're over thirty-eight, you'll know what I'm talking about. You taste modified foods, aka genetically engineered foods.

While taking a colonic for the first time, I was told a big parasite passed through. It could be seen through the glass tube. The alleviation I felt was immediately euphoric. I could suddenly climb up and down staircases. I needed no coffee to bounce off the walls. I lost weight, especially around my stomach.

I'm hoping that my story can inspire others to live longer. I am hoping that someone would get their lives together and not depend on dialysis. Even if I was too far gone in 2005, I am here today in 2007 still not on dialysis. Maybe this will inspire someone to be more disciplined. The more we take control of our gut, the more independent we become.

As you can see, I have self esteem issues. I was denigrated from early on. People don't realize that the bigotry mentality lives on in people through neighbors, teachers and preachers. The language itself was designed to enslave a person mentally. Words like denigrate, kinks, black magic, were designed to cause self-hate. Even as children we hear that Black people have bad hair and white people have good hair. The slave masters created these conditions deliberately, so that when you are set free, you are still mentally enslaved. I was told I was the ugliest person on the planet. Many people ask me if I am African. Now I realize it is a jealousy thing. They wish they had melanin. They wish they were the first and last. They wish they had access to the akhashic record. My genes are so ancient, I am closer to God. The first Adam created was a living soul. I have soul. The second Adam was a quickening spirit. The second creation was soul-less. He went as quickly as he came. How long have Black people been on the land developing civilizations after civilizations? Did they not work around the environment? How long have Europeans been on the planet? How many trees have they cut down? I have been very patient, putting up with their racial slurs. Some of them have the nerve to think racism has died. Let any Black person tell what it is like to be Black. It is like starting the race with one arm tied behind your back [and a foot, too]. So now we must rid ourselves from these toxins put out by automobiles and other by-products of the Industrial Revolution.

The Wonders of Clay

Ancient Africans, Afro-Americans, and dark people everywhere have always used clay. Please refer to the bibliography [Afro-Americans and Health]. Once you read the section on clay you'll understand the scientific explanation as to why clay has worked so well for many others and me. Some say it is the calcium and other minerals in the clay that gets your body back in top-notch shape. At first I did not know the reason. I just knew I felt better. Then as I was almost finished with this book I ran into that particular chapter. So now I know it was not my imagination or anyone's imagination. There is a scientific explanation behind the good feelings! Most people that suffer from kidney dysfunction and many other dysfunctions have a lack of calcium as one of the problem areas. The problem is many people are not even aware that they have a calcium deficiency. Furthermore, those who do become aware of the problem do not know how to correct it. They think they are doing right by buying store- bought supplements.

Many people use store bought calcium supplements thinking these products are real calcium. The body can tell the difference between calcium made in a lab and real calcium. Once you know how to buy natural calcium, you're well on your way to improving your health. CKLS and Clay get rid of potbellies. Red clay made my stomach go flat. I tell you, it expels gas while detoxifying. **<u>Sacred Woman</u>** author, Queen Afua, believes in clay as a healer. I took it and rubbed it on the outside of my belly and it helped. What I should have done is find out if she offered internal clay. Sometimes the ancestors come to me in dreams and tell me what to take. Okay, everywhere you go, the temperature is controlled.

You hop from home office and car. Each area is either air conditioned or heated. This works to your disfavor. In times past, and in some cases, the present, people still walk vigorously at the age of ninety. Sometimes they even work. The saying "hard work never killed anyone" was not referring to stress. It was referring to moving your muscles! Did you know that muscles atrophy when they are not used? Watch out for disease, if you are sedentary. A sit down job will do you more harm than good. Patients that lay in bed a lot have to be periodically moved for this reason. It is known to people well traveled that age has nothing to do with physical condition. Exercise in and of itself is a fountain of youth. Or should I say movement itself. Some people find pleasure in dancing. That is their form of movement. Whatever you do, get your groove on. Speaking of groove, I got my groove on at the Hip Hop dancing class at La Fitness. It was "the bomb," as the youth would say. I like the bicycle, while watching TV on the monitors, running and doing stomach lifts, with various machines. I do not recommend you plunge into a full workout without stretching or taking it slowly. Slow down. Do you talk faster than you can think? Do you sleep faster than you can wink? If you said yes, you're out of sync. Guess who said that? Me! It's part of my poetry passion.

I Love the Power of Clay!

One of the first signs that alerted my body that something was wrong was a dark lump that stuck out of my right side. For whatever reason, no doctor could figure out what was wrong before. So by the time I discovered the lump, I had given up on conventional doctors. I would go to doctors when the pain was unbearable. Otherwise, I prefer to stay away from them.

I heard Queen Afua was coming into town and she had a reputation for being a holistic healer. I went to the seminar, bought the green clay and applied it externally. I couldn't afford to buy anything else that day. The clay worked! The ugly dark lump that hurt, disappeared almost instantaneously. Clay made a believer out of me. One day I saw red clay at the natural food Co-op. I noticed they had both external application clay and internal clay, which removes toxins. I read the accompanying literature, stating that it acts like a magnet. I thought, "magnets are natural, earth is natural, there's something there." There is nothing like healing with earth, wind and fire. Please don't forget water. I have been using the clay ever since. I told everyone about it. They had me bringing the clay to work. I thought, "don't they consider it takes gas to drive 50 miles each time someone wants a jar?" I announced my healing modalities at a networking party. Everyone wanted it. Mind you, I had other things to sell. I became a distributor that day. And why not? I can't run all over the place buying people stuff. So the clay and the salt are now available at my store along with the usual shae butter, oils and incense. I tried tracing Queen Afua, but it was not easy without a computer. I was once again computer-less after the chronic illness ordeal at work left me practically homeless and business-less. So I stuck with local people's remedies, co-ops, and buying herbs in bulk. Essentially, it was the cheap-o way to go. So thanks to the mini-stroke, the long absence, the sexual harassment at work and my losing the EEO case. Due to these trials and tribulations I was able to figure out a way to heal me cheaply. Thanks to Malachi, Dr Sebi, Queen Afua, Dick Gregory, Elijah Muhammad, Adamah, Dr Sebi, Dr Llaila Africa and God, I was already on the right track. It was just a matter of mustering the guts to be disciplined and doing some research. Getting rid of a kidney problem when it's this far gone can take a while. It took years to create this problem so it's no over-night get well quick thing.

I later learned that you could also douche with clay and do an enema. Doing the enema with this red clay reminded me of the colonic I had done, where all that gook came out. Everyone should have at least one colonic. You breathe better. Doing an enema with this particular red clay made me breath better. More gook than ever came out compared to all other enema's I have previously done. I was sold even more.

Ginger Helps to Metabolize Foods

I had become "fat" in certain areas. Many will disagree. But if you stretch my fat at the arms, you'll see what I mean. Now it's different, of course. I am proud of the way my body has been sculpted by eating more vegetables, fruits and exercising. But exercise is only part of it, read on to see how I changed my diet. It was no over-night sensation either.

Ginger helps to metabolize foods. It is recommended for renal problems and dizzy spells. I took it for the dizzy spells and nausea unknowing that it was good for the kidneys. Some things just go together. You take something for one thing and you wind up treating more than one symptom.

Exercise

My bones had become so hollow; I was diagnosed as having too much bone loss. I found out later that you could increase bone mass by simply exercising! So the whole calcium drink milk theory is bogus! The lobbyist under self-interest re-directed people's thinking. This is how my Mom and aunt came to believe in the American food pyramid. We are constantly bombarded with ads on TV. Got milk? I hope not. In fact, I hope you turn off your TV. I pity the misguided children most of all. Some are very gullible. In fact, some children won't believe their parents. They think we are stupid. They think we are idiots that crawled out of a rock. Sadly, they will be the feeble ones with osteoporosis and Alzheimer's diseases. Stop the madness! Let's be a village all over again. You help my children and I will help yours.

Befriend an Animal

Animals are very special. They guide you and me. Listen to the little voice. It may be your higher self, trying to tell you something. It may be your ancestor. It may be God. It may be an angel. The difference between animals and us is that animals listen to the little voice. They readily interact with other dimensions, whereas humans have lost that skill. I have had help from the plant kingdom, the mineral kingdom [brown and neon colored minerals, crystals, and diamonds]. They have come to my rescue. All I have to do is listen. My higher self came out of me to get my attention, but I suppressed her and let the ego dominate. The insect kingdom came to my rescue, grasshoppers, butterflies, ants, and mammals came to my and rescue. Birds came to my rescue, owls and eagles. I was able to communicate with these beings. Have you noticed how intelligent animals are? They not only have personalities, but they are very aware of your feelings. Furthermore, they will not eat that which is bad for them, especially cats.

But cats will eat meat. Animals that eat meat are slower than those who do not. Small and large cats take more naps than animals that are vegetarians. True vegetarian athletes perform better than those who are not (7). Vegetarian people take fewer naps than meat-eaters. I am not referring to starch eaters who eat white flour products a lot pretending to be vegetarians, as Queen Afua's son would say. I'm talking about those who have discovered that in nature there is an abundance of vegetables and act upon it.

What Bitter Herbs Can Do For You

Here is how herbs came to my rescue, CKLS forces whatever is in you to come out. Worms come out because they hate bitters. The same is true for aloe vera resin. Some people don't want to acknowledge the vitamin content of herbs, but it is there. God said some plants are medicinal and others were invented as "meat." I tried dill because it is reputed to be good for urine and anti-inflammatory. One thing I noticed is that those that taste like licorice tends to be good for kidneys and milk production for women. These are fenugreek and dill. The ones that have estrogen are good for the prostrate such as saw palmetto. That's just an observation.

Green Plants; Detox and Oxygen

At some point I realized that we must eat more green things. Spinach is not the only green thing. People with kidney problems should stay away from spinach because it has oxalates. Thus, it produces kidney stones. I should have known there was something strange about it. The taste is strange. But a sister insisted it was good for you because she read it somewhere. Thus begun my eating spinach and cheese just before I entered college. So as you can see, I abandoned my ancestor's ways just before and during college. We struggle to become independent but we go about it the wrong way. Eventually, I replaced spinach with broccoli, cilantro, parsley, green peppers and salads in general. This is all recent behavior modification. The Bible says green herbs were created as meat for men and women. If you look at cilantro and parsley, they are seasoners that look like herbs, yet are high in nutrition. I cannot decide if they're herbs or vegetables or both.

I won't be surprised if God was referring to cilantro when he said plants are your meats. Someone did say manna tastes like cilantro. Just the fact that the Bible mentions an herb in a good light should be enough to make you want to use it. It's already in our tradition. How about yours?

The Starch Myth

The preservatives I encountered in my college days left my body wanting more; craving for minerals, and vitamins. As I researched through the years I found out about the superiority yucca has over potatoes; the vitamins, the minerals and especially the calcium, and the fiber. No wonder our teeth didn't fall out. Yautia, and name [pronounced nyame] all have manganese, magnesium, and great potassium ratios to calcium! No wonder our teeth didn't fall out despite the fact that cows milk is not part of our culture. Amazing how our ancestors had the right diet! All these are rich in fiber, especially coconut. Which reminds me, let me go eat some coconut.

Coconut made my teeth white and the white of my eyes even whiter. I resembled a model, great for a teeth commercial. My cousin still has those pictures. I don't know why he doesn't just let me have them.

As an alternative to meat I tried soy products. But then, I wondered just how much fiber was in these foods. It is still a processed food. Could my system be compromised because of this? Folks, I tell you, there is nothing like the diet of our ancestors. No lard was used, no strange oils, just olive oil, and apple cider vinegar with olive oil for dressing. Olive oil gets rid of gallstones. One person got mad when I mentioned olive oil, attributing this product to White Italians, which is totally incorrect. This is ignorance. Dark peoples have been using olive oil for eons! Why are Americans so brainwashed? Furthermore, it was the dark peoples that gave their cultures to Greeks and Italians and not vice versa. Wake up little people, wake up.

More Secrets of Fiber

Did you know coconut is 75 percent fiber? The lies about coconut oil are very disturbing. Another devil trying to block truth, I suppose. Do not follow the media for your information. One day something is good for you, the next day it's not. Go directly to the source. The village healers, the old cultures tell a lot. The people who live a long life tell a lot. There are some people that do not want to live a long time, because they feel sick right now. But little do they know, my people have not only lived a long time, they live a quality of life unsurpassed by modern folks and without wrinkles, thank you. As a matter of fact, it was in our islands that they thought they had discovered the fountain of youth. If you look at my 65 year old wrinkleless young looking cousin, looking like she's thirty, you'll understand why the conquerors thought there was a fountain of youth. My great aunt was 120 years old when she passed, with all her senses intact. My 94-year-old aunt has all her senses intact to this day. She has a better memory than most people. Have you noticed islanders's hair don't gray as much as other people? And neither do Chinese or Mexican's. It's the diet. They eat a lot more greens than you. This includes tea like oregano and seasonings like cilantro.

Parasite Killers & Fiber

Coconut has more fiber than every fiber food combined. Fiber affects mineral absorption. It controls blood sugar and gets rids of parasites, including invisible ones. Did you know that 90 percent of tapeworms are expelled after you eat coconut within 72 hours? Shame what happens to us when we stray from the mother diet. Figs and dates also have a great deal of fiber.

Let's take a look at the roles these foods and herbs play in the role of nutrition and health. Wormwood and walnut, which I take, kill parasites. I added coconut to the list because coconut gets rid of the invisible ones too, including gardinia. I was not going to stop at parasite extraction station, the colonic. What makes you think these critters aren't going to come back once you go back to your poor eating habit? We ordered fast food fried chicken for our brother's funeral. The worms became visible before we finished eating it. So I thought hmn, "I wonder how long that sat there before they served it to us?" And what happens to meat that is heated all day long? Makes you think twice about eating at fast foods. How much preservatives are in it? Once I made tea out of these powder forms of wood and nuts, the sugar was defeating the purpose. So, like the Chinese, I had to cut sugar or eliminate it from tea altogether. Sugar wreaks havoc in our immune system, while aggravating diabetes. I learned of the close relationship of diabetes and kidney disease as time went on. I rubbed the hardened portions below my breasts and above my stomach with grape seed oil, clay tea tree oil, and oregano oil. But, we were taught to use one herb at a time, not necessarily making too many mixes, lest they cancel each other out. Did I mention that coconut balances your sugar level?

Avoid Vices

People with kidney problems should stay away from chocolate, alcohol and coffee. Those are the three no no's. As a child I knew to stay away from chocolate. It did not taste right and made my stomach hurt. It seems that children have more common sense than adults. Later, I saw everybody eating chocolate and I thought, there was something wrong with me. If you are in the advanced stages, you should reconsider that cake you are about to eat. Why? Because it is essentially white flour, so it's fiber-less gunk completely devoid of nutrients. Imagine how long it takes to digest. Have you ever seen how cheesy meals stay stuck to the enamel of the toilet? White flour does the same thing. As a matter of fact, certain glue is made from it. I finally, gave up white flour.

KV, a medical technician gone holistic discouraged me from eating peanuts after finding out my condition and what I was trying to do. He didn't have to twist my arm because peanuts always gave me headaches. Headaches are the body's way of warning you that you have a food allergy. Interesting how our bodies speak to us. Chocolate also would give me a headache. I grew up hating chocolate bars, chocolate ice cream, chocolate pudding and chocolate cake. It's as if my body instantly knew. I suggest you listen to your bodies. I listened for a good part of my life. Why I caved in? I don't know. I felt bad saying no to family and friends. In some cultures, including mine, it is am insult to turn away someone's offer of food. Food offers are their way of showing you that they love you. I make people mad to this day when I go home to visit and turn down food. I guess there should be exceptions. Or maybe I should dunk the food when they aren't looking.

I love my Mom, but she will over-feed you. It is her way of showing love. Don't get me wrong. She did not have ideas about fatness being healthy until she came to this country. You should see how skinny she used to be. Also, she bought into the pyramid food ideology about how much meat and milk to ingest. When I saw the amount of dairy in the pyramid table, I should have known something was up. Later I found out that the lobbyists keep dairy before our eyes deliberately. In fact, they are behind the textbooks in schools, so of course, they can put what they want in them. This is their perfect chance to advertise. Sadly, many people bought into this food pyramid misconception. All peoples who live a long life and come to the States shorten it by adopting the American diet. Unfortunately, life is shortened within one generation. So, ladies and gentlemen eating correctly is a must. No one is safe from over-eating.

Here is a poem I wrote called "Sugared." By this time I was tired of being served sweets by colonizers. They come to your country serving over-processed stuff that has zero nutritional values. If that is not the devil in disguise, what is? Why would anybody try to break your body down like that? A people that don't bother anyone should not be subjected to foods that kill. But then again, the devil is the devil. You can call it what you want, but if it's not from God, it's the devil, said Neetta.

I wrote sugared around the year 2002. Want to kill the oldest, longest living animal in the world? Feed it sugar. That is the secret. Feed a crocodile white de-natured sugar and see what happens. You cannot force a cat to eat wrong. It won't let you. It is too smart. They are here to teach us.

SUGARED

SWEETLY SUGARED
COVERED IN FLAVOR
TOO OVERPROCESSED.
CAN YOU SEE WHAT LIES WITHIN?
WE SMILE AND HIDE THE PAIN WITH A GRIN.

PASTEURIZED, BLEACHED, HYDROGENATED
FLOUR, MILK, WHEAT
DID YOU IMAGINE
CHANGED TO WHO'S CONVENIENCE?
CAN'T FACE THE TRUTH, SO YOU LIVE A LIE?
WHOSE LIE?
ACCEPTANCE WITHOUT QUESTION
IS MEDIOCRITY FACING AN UNEMPOWERED SELF.

More Reasons to Avoid Sugar

The problem with sugar is that it causes too many diseases. Too much sugar can lead to diabetes, quiet as it is kept (8). Too much sugar can lead to renal failure as well. Too much sugar can lead to heart failure, cavities, the loss of bones period in your body, and other diseases. No wonder someone at the organic farm said, "sugar is the enemy." I believe sugar is one of the tests thrown at us by the enemy. Somehow sugar finds its way to third world countries where a lot of Blacks are. Today their health is becoming worst and worst. No one can dispute the fact that wherever modernity crops up, the life span diminishes in one way or another. Others don't realize that sugar can come from pasta, rice and other white flour by-products, in the sense that these products turn to sugar once inside the bodies. The worst part is these peoples did not eat pasta or white rice prior to the advent of foreign invasions. They ate cous-cous. But these "Middle Eastern" dishes had to be disguised as white rice to keep White people happy. Remember, we are talking about slavery and death. There was no choice. You can read about this. The black bean and rice, red bean and rice, all had a racial meaning to it. Ask anyone from the area. In fact, Moro is the name of a dish with red beans, to depict the dark peoples mixture with whites. The black bean dish represented black people and so on. Prior to the meeting of La Raza - the races, people used couscous. So now you see the origin of white rice. For some reason, White people wanted us to think that white is right, thus they created white foods, such as white rice, white flour, white sugar and so on to our detriment. The white potato replaced the yautia, yame/name, ahuyama and yucca [pronounced yooka]. The white potato has what appears to be zero fiber compared to the aforementioned. The lesson here is - do not pay attention to carbohydrates, pay attention to the type of carbohydrates and the fiber content. Complex carbohydrates are good for you. The afore-said have fiber, which is key, not to mention a host of vitamins and minerals not found in the white potato. Boy, have we been duped. Don't forget the white pasta. It is easy for me to wake up to the reality because I have lived abroad, and was raised in the original culture. This is why it is easier for me to discern. I must be patient with you all, considering the American way is all you know.

I suspect that nutricide is being done deliberately to eliminate Blacks because I look at the way Blacks were enslaved. One of the primary reasons for enslavement had to do with a need for people to pick sugar cane in the Caribbean Islands. Cotton picking came later. So, already, I suspect that sugar is behind this genocide tragedy. Only someone who has lived discrimination can relate to this. We know Aids was invented in a lab to eradicate Black people. We know that Whites tend to blame Africans for every disease when in fact; they were the ones who gave syphilis and gonorrhea to Blacks during colonial times. I have to look at the fact that small Black children are forced to be indoctrinated in school about European society, unnecessarily depriving them of their history. No other culture has been subjected to learning about themselves once a year in the shortest month of the year. So there is something very wrong with this picture.

A false diet has been imposed on people of African descent. It has also been imposed on people of hue all over the world. This is not a coincidence. This is a war. Black people all over the world are relegated to the lowest echelons. Look at the caste system in India. Go to any country and you'll see that the darker you are the more you are discriminated against. The dietary assault is no different. As sugar replaces honey, Stevia and other natural sweeteners, people's health condition changes. Diabetes of certain types can be triggered by diet. Studies after studies have proven that the more people adopt the Western diet, the more that diseases plague them. Latin Americans did not always eat white sugar. Today Black Latin Americans suffer with tooth decay like never before. This situation is not unique to Latin Americans, who now have the highest rate of diabetes than any other group. Needless to say they were influenced by Europeans and their obsession with sugar. Sugar and coffee were the major food crops forced upon Blacks by those who would enslave them. The French, and the Spaniards were particularly fond of sugar. The English were fond of meat eating. Some Europeans would drown the meat with alcohol consumption to make it digest. Alcohol attacks the purine in meats. But is it worth it? Not to me. The side effects are just not worth it. Another group that has been affected immediately by copying the Western diet is a group who lives in Nauru in the Pacific Island. So you see, no one is immune from the ill effects of a bad diet. The Western diet is rich in fats, sugar and meat. So it appears the Europeans brought their rich sorry diets with them to the New World, which was actually the Old world.

The World Health Organization conducted a study to confirm what I'm saying and the medical journals are full of them. They also confirm that the epidemic of diabetes is caused by lifestyle, not heredity. You will also notice the close relationship of diabetes and kidney disease. It is also noticeable that the same herbs that treat diabetes also treat renal conditions, though not always. You will also learn that many modern diseases, to include heart trouble, stroke and kidney disease are diet based in many cases. This means they are reversible just as I suspected. I only researched it this far to convince the skeptic. Prior to all this research, I had already conducted my own experiments. This means that the bibliography is for your sake, not mine.

Sugar or glucose damages the bloodstream. Too much sugar and meat can stress the body. When the body is forced to break down fats, it produces ketones, which are toxic. This toxicity leads to acidosis. The process of dehydration and high sugar levels stresses organs, including the kidneys. Your vision is impaired because certain arteries that connect to the eyes will be affected. The body has meridians that are connected. In the case of the kidneys, the right foot is part of the kidney meridian. Energy levels float in that direction. In other cases, damage to blood vessels that supply blood to the kidneys can cause permanent damage to the kidneys. So, there are many ways your kidneys can be damaged. If the arteries that lead to the brain are affected, you can have a stroke. The stroke can lead to Alzheimer's disease.

Sugar contributes to osteoporosis. Your bones become brittle and break easily due to mineral deficiencies. Sugar robs your body off minerals. It's bad enough we don't put minerals in our bodies. It's also bad that the foods are manipulated and genetically engineered, pasteurized and more. But on top of that you will eat something that robs your body off what little minerals there may be if any, that is quite a brainwashing feat. Or either it's a serious addiction. I hear that sugar is more addictive than cocaine. When you think of the world population and it's love affair with sugar, don't you just wonder?

Processed Foods

Processed foods, microwave dinners - modern marvels or spooky recipes? Processed foods affect how much we eat in that these are empty calories. Empty calories leave us craving for food, or at least we think so. But what the body is actually craving for is nutrient. If the microwave has killed what was left after all that processing then the quality of food is further affected. By the intense heat. It's bad enough the food has been processed and now we have to scorch it! This is called nutrition bankruptcy.

Harmful rays are at work. Do we listen to the elders? No. It took me a long time to get a microwave because we were taught better. For a long time my mother pleaded with me to allow her to give me the extra microwave. We didn't accept Christmas plates either. By this time she thought we were from another planet. It took me years to cave in, but eventually I did. Everything we did was different. We didn't celebrate monsters as dead ancestors for Halloween. We honored our ancestors not as monsters but for who they actually are. We venerate them. Well, back to my story. I accepted the microwave along with a bunch of other nonsense. The price of pleasing is not feasible just as I stated in my poem. People see that you are different and they want to break your code, not because they love you, but to tempt you. For example, I was led out of the community. But how many times did the beggars come visit me? Instead I had to visit them. So I say this to say, don't fall victim to people trying to socialize you into their lifestyle. It's usually to their benefit, your detriment. Alcohol is a perfect example of how friends try to socialize you into being "normal." Well everyone's body capacity is different. Did I mention sugar is processed with pig's blood? Alcohol has plenty of sugar.

Overcomingheavy Metal Poisoning

Kelp and alfalfa are some of the products I use when I want calcium in my body. A good overall food supplement is Emerald Blend. I use it for energy, balance, cartilage, to maintain normal blood sugar, and so on. It has MSM, green algae [which also detoxifies], copper, iodine, manganese, cobalt, selenium other sea minerals etc. These are Earth's essential elements. Selenium is a known detoxifier, particularly for people with kidney malfunction. Most people with kidney conditions are facing heavy metal poisoning. Sometimes I take selenium supplements by themselves. Other times I take the sunshine cleanse, which also has it. It has a lot of ingredients that get rid of heavy metals. Everyone with kidney problems has heavy metal poisoning. Even the water you drink has chemicals and heavy metals. This reminds me that a person with kidney problems should not drink tap water for that very reason. They should instead drink distilled water. Spring water has some natural metals according to some. So distilled water is recommended even when you take the internal detoxifying clay. The distillation process gets rid of the heavy metals. The idea is to cleanse, so let's keep it real. If possible, you should have a filter throughout your house, so you won't have to cook with or shower with poisonous water. The best filter is the wellness filter. No monetary connection there, just free advertising for www.wellnessfilter.com.

Chapter 8

The Price of Good Health

I was still determined not to take poisons [legal drugs]. Some of the names of the drugs, I cannot pronounce. Some were antibiotics. Others were painkillers. There were some diuretics. Others helped control the blood pressure. I hear that controlling the blood pressure only masks a greater problem. Then I wondered about the warnings on the label. The warning alone was a book unto itself, just as you see on Saturday Night Live parody. I thought the TV characters were exaggerating at first. Then I actually read the instructions. It is scary enough that they keep stuff from you. But then to have them confess it, you know something is wrong. But it wasn't the warning signs that actually scared me. I was invincible, after all, or so I thought. What really scared me were the actual side effects I was feeling. Pharmaceuticals had me moving in slow motion. Then, they blame the patient and throw in another drug to eliminate the side effect caused by the other drug. And so on. Until you say, enough!

I still recall what over-the-counter painkillers did to me. The side effects were ugly. I never again touched Advil after that. It nearly killed me. I guess poison plus poison equals danger. Why treat a poisoned system with poison? Drugs are created in a chemical lab. There is nothing natural about it. Let's face it, we now know legal drugs came from herbs. Painkillers come from meadow root, white bark, cherry bark pineapple and yucca. Parts of the pineapple are also used as digestion aid, just as parts of the papaya [lechosa] are utilized for their digestive enzymes.

Healing with Real Salt -The Price of a Miracle Cure

Salt comes from pink or gray minerals in the ocean. They are processed to become poisons. Do not use table salt. And that was my undoing. Our people did not escape to the health food stores. They just took what was sold to them at face value. But we know better nowadays. Get your miracle salt from the health food store. Let it be pink in the form of a rock. In Georgia, you can get it from Sevananda or Life's Essentials. This natural phenomenon has everything the bodyneeds in proportions conducive to proper bodily development, compared to coffee, which tends to stunt your growth. I was told the story of who had a breast lump to disappear after cutting out coffee altogether. The person that told me this story was sipping on a cup of coffee. I looked at the cup and she must have read my thought. "The coffee habit is hard to break," she confided. "But I am cutting down," she continued.

I had heard enough. Coffee and alcohol cause water retention. What a surprise. I was a coffee drinker during the episode. So, I too, had to cut back. I also wonder if it's the amount of coffee. As I go back to visit the Kiskeya, I notice the coffee cups are not coffee cups at all. They are the size of an espresso cup. Have you seen one? It's like drinking one-third the size of a small cup. Someone once told me you could eat anything as long as you eat it in small portion or flush it with water. I don't know about all that. True you should flush with water [if nothing else to avoid water retention]. I wouldn't go as far as to say eat anything. I certainly won't eat any more scavengers. Warning ! Warning! High cholesterol! Heavy metal poisoning! But as far as coffee, Latin-American cultures and Eastern cultures drink small portions of coffee and swear it helps with metabolism. True, it is acidic. But, remember, these peoples eat a lot more vegetables and fruits than you. I wonder if Europeans forced Blacks to work the coffee field in a deliberate attempt to ruin their health. After all, look what happened with sugar.

Start a Farm

Straying from our ancestors diet can prove deadly. Kwanza brings us back in touch with our ancestors. It was originally a root festival. Celebrating earthly grown roots- -a harvest so to speak. In my culture, we celebrate the harvest in the fall. Farmers bring together the crops they each grew and share under one roof or yard so that all have larger portions of a feast. How resourceful. I spoke about the wonders of yucca and name [pronounced nyame]. Then there is platano [plantain]. Plantains have been associated with urine in that it stops bedwetting. They also address urinary tract infections.

Purify

I finally got rid of the bulge with internal red clay by Mother Earth' Blessings. At some point I realized, you cannot nourish a body that is toxic. After the colonic, I took the clay, blood purifiers, and heavy metal removers. Once the blood is compromised no amount of nutrients will do you any good. You will always be hungry. Always being hungry even after you eat is a sign that something is wrong. Clean plus dirt equals dirt. Nutrients plus toxins equal toxins. So, eating period, no matter how healthy I ate, was a waste of time. Once I realized this, I began to purify the blood using burdock and sorrel with and without ginger. Then I tried to kill the parasites using walnut hulls, dark and powdery. I also graduated to wormwood pills from the health food store, in conjunction with cloves, which also are a cleanser, and anti microbial. People, people, people - did I not tell you our ancestors from Atlantis were right on the money? Check yourself before you reject a culture. The culture you reject may just be your own. I knew the parasites don't disappear overnight with one colonic. If after a colonic you eat meat, they are there. Who? The parasites return. And also too much sweets will bring them on. I also recall they cannot stand the taste of green seed called pumpkin seed. So I ate a lot of that. Even people at work were joining the bandwagon. They know their health is at stake. They know how they feel, though at first they resist. Eventually they come around. Now everyone is begging me to write a book. They see my skin clearing. They see my stomach shrinking. They note I did not go conventional. Nope, I did not even succumb to dialysis. I spit out remedies out the top of my head without having to look it up and they are impressed. I can tell you right off the bat oregano has oil in it that is anti-microbial. No wonder my people are never out of these products (cloves, ginger, oregano). Once you find out how powerful they are, you'll never be without them either. Cheap does not mean ineffective in this case.

Resins

I used to be so impacted my stomach bulged. Often, I was asked if I was pregnant. I would get full quickly and couldn't ingest food. When I began throwing up as predicted by the doctor along with the metallic taste in mouth, that's when I knew I was in trouble. Not to mention my urine was coming out sideways. Supposedly if you don't sit straight for fear of public toilets, you compromise one kidney. Who knows? All I know is I was caught up in it and was I was in trouble. Fasting didn't help digest food. It just sat there for days, months, and years. It was time to do something about it. I began to smell like a corpse. I began to smell like the carcass I was eating. Folks, you smell like what you eat. If you eat snot, I mean cheese, then you smell like mucous. And so on. I decided I wanted to smell like Frankincense, so I ingested it. I wanted to smell like sandalwood so I ingested it and so on with amber resin and other good smelling resins. Well read it for yourself. The benefit of ingesting the aforementioned is astounding! It has everything to do with eliminating kidney problems, so I was on the right track! While chaste berry and pure cranberry along with tart cherry, blueberry and pomegranate helps, the scented resins are a Godsend.

The More Expensive Herbs

Kidney problem and its cousin, diabetes can result from high blood pressure in the case of kidneys and or sugar poisoning. Don't laugh at sugar. Sugar has been known to cause heart attacks, as the kidneys are damaged from high blood pressure. High blood pressure is the body's way of coping with a stressed system...a loaded system. So as high blood pressure damages the kidneys, toxic waste builds up, resulting in a coma and even death. Keep playing with your health and you'll pay with your life. "The wages of sin is death"...that is what that meant. Parsley has become my best friend. It cleans the liver. It is good for digestion, and has chlorophyll. Parsley is another blood purifier!

Now they're selling products with hydrangea and dandelion to cure kidney disease. Did I not take hydrangea before? Yes. It increases the flow of urine. It is a diuretic. But I stopped, and took it for granted along with dandelions. See because it was too cheap. Come on, something that grows wild in your backyard is good for you? A weed? Ladies and gentlemen, dandelion removes toxins from the kidney, and is a diuretic. I began to recall the American Indian Festival where dandelions are praised. I no longer look at the price of things. If it works, it works, expensive or cheap. But as far as your health, you can't put a price tag on it. If something costs $125.00 for a one-day toxic metal removal, I would take it if it works for many people, because as I said before, health is priceless. Willy, the visionary dream-maker is no longer with us. I wonder what would have happened to his life if he had gone alternative early on.

Get Hip to the Mineral Absorption Game

Amino acids and fiber help with mineral absorption. Somewhere down the line I found out fiber affects mineral absorption. This means that people whose diet is poor in fiber are in danger of being mineral deficient! Here comes coconut to the rescue again. No wonder our people worship the coconut! It saved my teeth where there was no cow' s milk. My sisters ask me why my teeth haven't fall out since I always ate more sweets than anyone else. I tell them because I was in love with coconut. It's been proven to help teeth from falling. Coconut is loaded with calcium. Also the high fiber content help with mineral absorption. So guess who went back to eating coconut? You guessed it. If you want tapeworms and other parasites to leave you, just eat what parasites hate. They hate coconut, walnut, wormwood, pumpkin seeds and anything bitter. I was doing the opposite one time eating sweets. The thing is, my Mom told me if I ate too many sweets, I would get parasites. How do these people know all these things with just a third grade education? The parasites come out of your stool. You may not see it but they are there. All Americans have it. All meat eaters have it. All sweet tooth people have it.

Bee Pollen

Bee pollen is a godsend, for it has lysine or cystine or phenylalamine. Ladies and gentlemen, these are the building blocks of life. It has been proven that cells saturated with bee pollen can clone themselves in the right environment. This information has been known for some time, but kept from the general public. The status quo wants you to self-destruct, instead. They allow the sale of nicotine and animal products knowing the animal leaves a little bit of himself in you. The plant kingdom does not do that. It leaves vitamins and minerals, but not toxins. Animals are the only ones that leave toxins in your body. They also leave bad cholesterol in you.

Let's see, after the Flood people begin to eat meat. Put two and two together, and you, solve that puzzle yourself. Let's see, the cave man, uncivilized resorted to cannibalism. Disease was introduced at this time. Let's see, Africans (to include Egyptians [same people]) did not include treatment for heart disease or cancer, diabetes or kidney disease in their medical manuals. Why not? These diseases did not exist! You are witnessing modern phenomena. These diseases are modern marvels. They especially appeared in high numbers after meat consumption became a part of everyday life. These diseases increased during the Industrial Revolution. After the turn of the century is when people really began to exaggerate meat consumption on a worldwide level. Communication between Europeans and the rest of the world improved at this time. Thus, their influence worldwide was felt more than ever.

Sugar eliminates minerals out of your system. It is important to take minerals because without minerals, teeth become very thin and they start to crack. Next thing you know you have all kinds of crowns for your teeth and you may even find yourself teeth-less. You may also notice knees and hips hurting. These are your bones deteriorating, thinning out! You are mineral, you are salt. You are what you eat and where you come from. All life emanates from the sea. So when we say drink Irish moss. Don't think yucky. Think of all the minerals that are in such a natural milkshake. It is drunk all over Jamaica. They make it taste good with soymilk, ginger or whatever you decide to put in it. They use isinglass and flax. Your body needs nothing else after that. Flax alone in liquefied form is a demulcifier. It is great for absorbing bacteria in the intestines. The same is true for marshmallow root. Do not turn up your nose at anything that is baboso. The slimy okra in gumbo has a similar effect.

More Bee Pollen Please

Bee pollen is rich in protein. But some would rather get protein from animals that may not only be malnourished, but may come from unsanitary processing plants. Some of these animals are diseased and are used for hot dog making and hamburger making and you know it. This is nothing new. But fear of being an oddball keeps you enslaved to do as the Romans. Face it, we all did it. But let's break the chain. You now know better, so you should do better. Kidney disease comes about from eating too much protein. Whatever the other reasons, why add fuel to the fire? Bee pollen has higher levels of amino acids than those of animal origin; 19 percent to be exact. Now compare that to meat's 16 percent. Meat has 1.28 percent leucine compared to bee pollen's 5.6 percent.

Rutine, a glucoside classified as vitamin P or R is found in bee pollen. It helps with the intellect, cerebral hemorrhage and the heart in particular, according to Dr. Felix Murat's findings through research. The mineral content of bee pollen includes potassium, magnesium, calcium, copper, iron, silica, phosphorus, sulphur, chlorine [not disproportionate by the way [, and manganese. Mankind is the one who goes around providing elements in disproportion to that found naturally in the Earth.

You don't have to wait until you are completely cured to eat bee pollen. In fact, you will need bee pollen for energy while your body is depleted or loaded down with heavy metals and food toxins. Bee pollen is the same ingredient found in concenergy. No other vitamin or supplement works quite like it. From the author's experience, the energy is immediate. Before you say you are allergic to pollen, let me assure you that it is not the same pollen in the air. The bees do not use that for their young. There are two kinds of pollens and bees use only the best. The pollen pushed around by the wind from the trees is the anemophile pollen. Those are pushed by the wind and stem from willows, oaks, conifers and others. The type I am talking about is entomophilies and these are the types bees collect. The bees are no dummies. They would not dare give their young something harmful. You should learn a lesson from them. These pellets are sticky, not airborne. If anything, this type of pollen has an immunizing effect, so let's get the record straight. Bee pollen cures many diseases, to include kidney disease. It is fascinating that I was taking it just for the vitamin content alone, not to mention energy. But as if that wasn't enough, bee pollen has everything the body needs to duplicate itself. Every so often cells renew themselves. Just as a snake sheds skin, humans also shed skin and renew themselves, provided they eat right. If humans eat animal by-products, disease ensues and the aging process begins. People say you begin to die the minute you begin to live. But consider this. People used to live to 900 years or more. The people of Africa, to include Egypt, were found as mummies with bee pollen still in their gut. This means that eating bee pollen is nothing new. It has been recently rediscovered, when it was noticed that beekeepers lived longer than the general populace. No doubt, they partook of that which they reaped. Bee powder has nutritive and medicinal values.

What is the composition of bee pollen? Bee pollen has an impressive amount of nitrogen, such as proteins, minerals, amino acids and trace elements. It also contains vitamins, hormones, rutine and anti-biotic properties. These miraculous elements are hard to find in regular foods. People nowadays obtain nourishment from animal sources, yet these animal sources don't have half the content of what bee pollen has. Animal protein in particular, comes with a heavy price. Along with it come fats that are hard to process. The animal may or may not have eaten properly, so they may or may not lack nutrients.

Add the Goodies to Your Water

Do you want to decrease your chances of loosing your kidneys? Drink water. If you have an aversion to the way water taste, add lemon. In fact lemon is one of those healers where no disease can exist in its presence. So stock up on lemons! Not drinking enough water leads to a condition called edema. This is essentially water retention. Drinking celery juice should take care of this. For those who don't like it's taste, you simply mix it with apple juice. You might consider either getting a juicer or buy juices from the health food section and mix them as mentioned. You don't want to over-mix. Always take one herb at a time or one juice at a time; and mix only in cases where the flavor is too powerful or too whatever. In a revelatory dream I heard the elders say I should hydrate myself more if I wanted to have healthy organs. I was shown my organs versus another female organs that drank a lot of water. You should have seen how supple it looked. This was before I had seen real damaged organs versus supple organs. The thing with me is I see things before eye see it. ozonated water is worth investing in. The price difference is not that much compared to what it does. It adds oxygen to your system. You get oxygen at the cellular level. This is important for people with chronic illness because it is lack of oxygen that creates disease.

Stomach, pain, protruding belly, fatigue, bloating are all signs that there is disease in the colon. But whether it is caused by Irritable Bowel Syndrome or not, your kidneys are stressed. The point here is that if your kidneys are affected, then you must address each root cause. Yes bad breath and metallic taste are all part of IBS as well as kidney disease. Have you noticed that these two go hand in hand, like what came first the chicken or the egg? Just rest assured that the alternative methods we're speaking of here addresses both issues.

Deep Tissue Massage

Another alternative method of healing is deep tissue massage. I bumped into deep tissue massage at the mall. There are chairs in the center, where you sit to be treated like a king or queen. The literature boasts of how certain types of massage will detoxify you and help with digestion. So you can imagine which one I chose, for only twelve bucks! If that is not an inexpensive way to heal I don't know what is. Think about it; most people pay an arm and a leg for massages, let alone deep tissue massage. I am here to tell you that you don't have to pay an arm and a leg. You can just go to the mall and have it done for $12.00. What's incredible is that the quality of the service is just like [if not better] than a Swedish massage. When you come out, you feel like a new person. Your body is in total orgasmic state. You feel healthier than ever. You breathe better. It is worth every penny! Deep tissue massage leaves the body relaxed, rested. You feel the benefits of the kneading, tapping, shaking. Your nerves and glands will thank you for it. The lymphatic drainage system is cleansed. The circulation is improved. You feel revived and energized. I took my daughter [just had to share] and she testified how much it was worth it. Somehow deep tissue massage filters bacteria and toxins. Toxins are removed, as in moved through the drainage system. Good-bye aches and pains. Waitresses and waiters really appreciate this. Deep tissue massage helps the body heal itself. You feel your craniosacral spinal column improve mobility, thereby increasing your range of motion. This is important because as we age, our range of motion is limited because of dis-ease, due to the way we eat. People who suffer from carpal tunnel, tennis elbow, bursitis or any job where repetitive motion is required, will benefit from deep tissue massage.

Educate Yourself as a Consumer

You will have to learn how to educate yourself. You must read labels. Pork is disguised as glycerin or lard. Corn syrup will lead to disease. Corn syrup is put in just about everything. It is merely sugar. What is passed off as juice is sometimes sugar water. In many cases, the juice contents is only ten percent, but sellers still call it "juice." Try not to consume foods with monosodium glutamate. One of the purposes [if not the only purpose] is to enhance the flavor of food. There is no nutritional content in this additive.

Overeating can slow down our metabolism and limit our range of motion. We become sluggish and wonder why we don't have energy. Think of how we tax the kidney, forcing it to process the unthinkable. Some call modern day foods "toxic soup" because it is ridden with chemicals, we can't even pronounce. Many people do not even read the label. This is what brought me to write "The Miseducated Consumer," a spoken word piece that did very well.

Being overly toxic leads to cancer. Doctors usually don't detect cancer until it is well into a so-called irreversible stage. Sometimes they catch it early, but not always. Some people do not go to doctors until it is too late. But what they don't know is that it is never too late. Speaking of "it's never too late," I wrote a song called "Times Are Trying" which won honorable mention at the Cotton Club in Atlanta, Georgia. I speak of how it's never too late to turn your life around. If people really want to heal they'll find a way naturally.

Solving Circulation Problems and Pain

I found out through research that Co-Enzyme Q10 transports oxygen to the circulatory system. People with heart trouble aren't the only ones who suffer with a circulation problem. Ever heard of PAD? I call it dead leg syndrome. You get to the point where you can't even drive, because your foot won't extend without excruciating pain. People with kidney dysfunction may have poor circulation anywhere in the body, particularly in the leg. The right leg is part of the kidney meridian.

Sufferers may have to take cayenne pepper and ginger to increase circulation. You can obtain the root at most American grocery stores. With the Spanish population increasing, you now have more foreign foods in the regular market. You can even find yucca, a painkiller, and right in your neighborhood grocery store. Blackberries are powerful painkillers as well. Yucca also has plenty of fiber, so I won't go by the name if I were you. It is also a good source of calcium and phosphorus. When you get a chance research the benefits of yucca and you'll see how it's superior it is to the potato.

Exotic Starch:
And Vitamins and galore

Some people think starch is a bad thing. But in actuality it is the type of starch that is a bad thing. If you're talking about macaroni and cheese, yes. But yucca, name [nyame], yautia and ahuyama are all starchy foods, but carry such a great amount of fiber. They are all wonder foods, with plenty of nutrition, vitamins enzymes and minerals. You now see them in pill form. That is usually a sign that it has crossed over and it is seen for the wonderful capacity it has. There is nothing wrong with starch so long as it has fiber and vitamins. In nature, food works synergistically. Processed white rice is not made by nature. Neither is macaroni. White rice, pasta and potatoes turn to sugar in your body. This does not help the diabetes epidemic. Kidney dysfunction and diabetes tend to go hand in hand. By the way, potato is not an original food. For further information see the works of Dr. Sebi.

Treat Acidosis

Eating affect the way you look. Free radicals make you look older. Free radicals are molecules that have been impaired and have to resort to stealing an electron from another molecule. This damages the cell. Everything is thrown out of whack, protein synthesis, tissue regeneration, organ repair and oxygen level. This entire process, which lowers oxygen level, scientifically, results in too much acid being produced. High acid state produces more free radicals, to the extent that it becomes a viscous cycle (9). Eighty percent of ill people suffer from acidosis. But they also have mucous. This is why some people say disease is mucous and others say its alkalinity versus acidity.

Inflammation follows, thus some say disease is inflammation. I say it is all the above. Lack of oxygen and so son - all parts affect each other. We were not created in a vacuum. You cannot treat one part and not the other. Always try to get to the root cause. Sugar will cause your skin to appear old and wrinkly. It also causes high blood pressure. Still want sugar? Did I tell you it causes pancreatic dysfunction? The blood becomes sticky. The arteries become clogged. Remember my dream about how the oldest animal in the world, the fearsome crocodile, can be killed by simply giving him sugar? I don't need scientists to tell me anything. I can access the akhashic records any time I want to. I did further studies after this book was written, for your sake, not mine. There are people that have to have the backing of professionals or scientists. Whether I was a scientist in another life may or may not be relevant to some, especially if you don't believe in reincarnation. What is funny is that the same people who claim not to believe in reincarnation believe that Christ rose again on the third day. So, back to sugar. Sugar attaches itself to protein. This produces a glue-like substance. This causes pressure. Your mitochondria are affected. Remember science class? This is where all the energy comes from. But now that you have damaged it, you feel fatigued.

So much for the sugar highs and why you come crushing down. This is a false sense of high. You cannot reach the Most High with false selections. You got to come naturally. You cannot create anything that has not been already created, nor can you duplicate it.

I have also noticed that what treats kidney disease also treats gout (10 see **Las Hierbas Que Curan**). Gout is caused by too much uric acid. When I went to see a specialist, I was told that I had too much uric acid in my urine. Meat eating causes too much uric acid. People with gout have problem with metabolism. But metabolism is not a disease unto itself. People damage their metabolism by the way they eat. It has been said that chronic anemia can also interfere with gout and metabolism. Eating organ meats, sausages, anchovies, crab, shrimp, milk, eggs, soybeans and other processed meats can give you too much purine. Gout can be caused by too much aspirin or commercial diuretics (11). Twenty five percent of gout cases are caused by these drugs (12). Ninety percent of gout sufferers have kidney stones (13). Just as I suspected, I found that one could treat arthritis, gout, diabetes and kidney disease by diet and detoxification (14). I am on the right track! Sometimes we eat too fast and do not digest foods properly. I was always accused of eating like a bird, too slow. That was a good thing. This American fast pace is not such a good thing. Americans eat fast, and sleep fast. Eating faster than you can digest means waste gets trapped. That is not good.

If your eyes are watery you may be suffering from acidosis. If white stuff comes out of your eyes you are overly acidic. The same is true of lower back pain. At some point you may have to go raw as in a raw vegetable diet, even if you know it's not going to last. Try it for a month for the sake of changing your body chemistry. You owe it to yourself and your loved ones to get healthier so you can be around to see the hereafter or make a difference. Once you go raw, you see that just about every disease disappears. Everyone in all different walks of life has had very positive results from a raw diet.

Oxygen to the Rescue

Flax seed also helps to regulate the flow of oxygen and nutrients. Other foods that help with oxygen flow are foods containing quercetine [such as red onions used by the original Indians], cat's claw [una del gato], and grape seed extract. Blue green algae repairs cells. Some people recommend cottage cheese and pineapples. But it is better to be off of dairy products altogether. You should avoid all flesh, if you really want to heal. When I got real sick and couldn't walk, that is what I did.

During the early part of my healing I used beets as a blood purifier because as you may know, kidney dysfunction has a lot to do with bad blood when blood becomes toxic due to heavy metals and other factors. I had also heard that beets have oxalates, which is not good for the kidneys. I never had trouble out of beets. Spinach also has oxalates, so kidney sufferers should never eat spinach. Find another way to purify the blood, such as using chlorophyll supplements or wheat grass. Wheat grass is the ultimate blood purifier. It not only cleanses your blood, but it serves as a great detoxifier. When you have kidney stones, you have chemicals in your urine. You need to eat a low protein diet at this point. Too much protein in your system will force your system to grow stones. Magnesium prevents stone formation. So do barley bran, oats and brown rice. These are considered transitional foods, until one gets to the point where one is eating nothing except raw foods. If you can afford it, go to a professional for oxygen treatment. They can put it in your blood. Or you may want to do it yourself by trying food grade hydrogen peroxide. Professionals give you quicker and more efficient results.

Fluoride Problems

Toxins are hard to avoid in a modern world where people are careless as to what they ingest and what beauty products they use. You can find toxins in toothpaste. Most commercial toothpastes have fluoride and lauryl sulfate. You can find a good calcium supplement made naturally at Dr Chris's pharmacy 1982 HWY 78 in Snellville, GA.

Charcoal addresses food autointoxication. Alternative toothpastes can be found in health food stores. Don't forget that fluoride is a heavy metal, found in both toothpaste and your water supply. As you brush, fluoride oozes down your throat and into your body cavity. When you study the story of how fluoride came to be in toothpaste you would understand that it's nothing but lobbyists trying to make a buck. Fluoride is a residual from chemical labs; a leftover from corporate processing plants. The body was not made to release heavy metals. Some people are proud of the sanitary water that is provided in the United States. But what they do not know is that too much chloride goes into the water supply. The purpose of putting chloride in the water supply is to eliminate microorganisms found in water that are dangerous to human health. Unfortunately, it is a hit or miss trap. The scientists themselves are not sure how much is too much. So, we, the public, aka guinea pigs suffer the consequences. No one is safe. Read about it on your own. Hit "chlorine in our water supply" or something like that and you will never drink tap water again. Nor will you bath in it. You won't even cook in it! How do you think healthy people with healthy habits suddenly get sick? Why do you think normal people are suddenly having kidney problems? Chances are, you know someone with a kidney condition. Even people who may not read this book know someone with kidney problems. Before I started writing this book, I had no idea kidney disease was such an epidemic. As soon as I would mention my book, someone would say they couldn't wait until I was finished with it. What is worst is that now people are being born with kidney disease. One doctor suspects I was born with a blocked stomach and that is what is causing the kidney problems. They do not know for sure, but they told me to see a specialist. I do not stop anyone from seeing a specialist. But I do encourage everyone to be a smart consumer. This includes picking doctors. You should consider getting a water purification system. If you cannot afford it, use cheesecloth and charcoal over your faucet.

Buy Organic

We are toxic because we trust what grocery stores sell us. Labs have gone as far as processing genetically engineered foods. When seedless fruits are introduced, you get unpredictable results. Playing God is no joke. Bacteria inside internal organs are a serious event. It was to this end that I wrote the poem, "Genetic Engineering." Lab crazy folks use fish and tomatoes and cross them over. What are we ingesting? What are we giving our kids? And we wonder why we are sick. When you eat organic, you are avoiding chemicals. I was once a pusher of organic eating, creating a newsletter called "Organic Times," and appearing on the radio speaking out against genetically engineered foods. I brought a lot of people into the Loganville farm and was heard throughout 89.3 FM radio station. I spoke about environmental pollutions and wrote "Sewer Sludge" which talks about the infamous toxic soup. I spoke out against vaccination. Vaccinations are - pus in your veins, plus heavy metals to include cadmium, lead, arsenic and mercury. Not surprisingly, they are mostly found in Black neighborhoods under the disguise of free care for the poor and the homeless. Fascinating that foods laden with the aforesaid heavy metals are sold in poor ghettos and wherever Black people live, be they middle class or poor. A place called Piggly Wiggly sold engineered foods as such. It was known to many that these engineered foods were processed with sewer sludge. That is what I had in mind when I wrote Sewer Sludge. If you buy organic from health food coops or health food stores, you won't have to worry about fish eggs in your tomatoes or frog legs in your asparagus.

More Heavy Metal Detox

Heavy metal and chemical toxicity takes years to develop in healthy individuals. But because of our modern lifestyle with sedentary jobs, we set the pace for our own destruction. In this lifestyle, we are exposed to fast foods, and pollution, just to name a few. You and I both know the kidney was not made to process chemicals such as are found in our modern world. Silver amalgam fillings contribute to elevated levels of mercury. Vaccines also have high levels of mercury, cadmium and lead. The chemical bombardment seems to be deliberate. The worst medical projects can be found in poor neighborhoods and wherever Blacks are. That is called "environmental racism." You can cleanse from heavy metals with mullein and marshmallow. Marshmallow is also great for people with kidney problems. It cleanses the kidneys. That is because mullein and marshmallow have a slimy reaction with water, along with fibers that make the intestines dance, as impurities wiggle their way out. I use dandelion leaf and olive leaf to address the cleaning of the kidney and keeping the blood pressure in check, respectively. The author of New Body feels that uva ursi help the kidneys as well. Sea vegetables help with heavy metal detox. Sea vegetables include, Nori, Bladder Wrack, blue-green algae, and brown algae. It won't hurt to take Kombu, Bucchu, and Irish moss.

There is a warning out now that says eat fish only once a month. That right there should tell us something is wrong with our waters being polluted to the point where you can't even eat fish. I had a dream once, just before they made the announcement about eating fish once a month only, where a fish was saying to me, "Don't eat me!" It was a telling dream, more like a revelation. Dreams sometimes tell me what to do. For instance, one dream told me to eat raspberries and purple lettuce in order to cure. At the time I thought I had liver problems. Well it turned out I had kidney problems and I found out later that red raspberries, blueberries and purple lettuce are good for kidney inflammation. Before the dream I had no way of knowing this since I am not a doctor [in this life]. Our ancestors try to communicate with us. Our ancestors may be part of the saints that have been venerated for years. My grandmother is one such saint. I couldn't even go into details of how much she has helped me. We have gotten away from the truth of instincts and how they work because society tells us not to follow hunches, gut feelings, instincts or dreams. We live in a world where the two dimensional thinking thwarts the real three-dimensional or multi dimensional realms. To this end I wrote the now famous poem "Soul Healing." A lot of my poems talk about healing, environmental issues and metaphysical ideals intertwined with spirituality.

Parasite Removal

Once we ingest toxic matter, it builds up in the colon [also known as the death chamber]. Here you have digested and undigested items as well as fungus and parasites. Because we don't let our digestive system rest, it is constantly working overtime. Fasting allows the digestive system to rest. Once we fast, we need to get rid of the culprit rather than adding more problems to the issue. In other words, we need to do colonics, then enema then ingest perfect nutrients such as bee pollen and wheat grass. All the supplements in the world won't help unless your colon is clean. For a long time I took products designed to have all the nutrients the body needs. The problem is it was not being absorbed because my colon was overloaded with toxins, heavy metals, parasites, and undigested fecal matter. The same is true for most people who suffer with kidney problems. So, think of detoxifying first before you get into any program. Aloe Vera has a bitter taste so it can act as a laxative as well. Many times you can create your own program through research and common sense. Get rid of your potbelly. Don't rely on commercial laxatives because they don't get rid of the problem. They make your intestines lazy and you simply become dependent on commercial laxatives. Try Cascara Sagrada, Senna and other natural laxatives such as castor oil [flavor it if you must].

Our ancestors knew what they were doing. Many of us have forgotten these practices. We allow others to rob us of our cultural practices, readily accepting a foreign culture that may not work. Wake up and smell the coffee. What is really brewing? What is really brewing is capitalists trying to make a buck, and superiority complex people are running rampant, devouring whom they may. Let your body's reaction be the judge. Be more in tune with your instincts. To this end I wrote the poem, "Instincts." We often forget about the nutrient absorption cycle. We forget there is decay; permanently turning off the switch of common sense. We forget about how our ancestors ate and how strong they were or how long they lived. We forget that we used to eat a light meal at six, called supper; and never ate past seven. We forget melanated peoples built the pyramids. Bee pollen was at the base of their diet, along with garlic and other goodies.

We don't realize how we are stressing our immune system, or our circulatory system. We eat items that cause plaque build up. White flour clogs your arteries just as bad as meat. Any time you clog your system, you are asking it to shut down, whether it be the circulatory system or the lymphatic system or any system of your body. A stroke is simply a shutting down of blood or oxygen to the brain. A heart attach is an impediment of blood to the heart. You see where I'm going with this? All systems in the body are interrelated. So don't neglect a portion of you because you will live to regret it. I also used Co-Enzyme Q10, which is a great detoxifier.

You could also try eating pumpkin seeds for parasite removal. Helpful herbs are wormwood and walnut hull powder. Bitter herbs help. And don't forget my good friend, the coconut. Coconut is more effective because it addresses all the various categories of parasites.

Colonics

Some professionals that do colonics suggest adding hydrogen peroxide [not the commercial kind of course - the food grade kind] to the water during a colonic irrigation. This is a good idea because your colon laden with putrefication is suffering from lack of oxygen. Irrigations help control blood pressure. I noticed my blood pressure had improved after the colonic. This makes sense. Colonics with ozonated water helps restore the PH balance of the colon. It breaks down body odor of course. Some people can be smelled a mile away. Some people have no idea how bad they smell, or how sick they are. Some people's bowel movement is sticky and hard to flush. These are the white rice, white flour eating no drinking water individuals. They eat cheese and so on. If your stool is not long round and smooth, you got issues in your digestive tract. My colonic costs me $80.00 without ozone.

Hydrotherapy in the form of a colonic is an internal bath of the part of your body and where all disease originates. It removes waste from the colon. If you have old fecal matter in your system, which refuses to pass, you may experience headaches. People truly express relief after a colonic because they truly didn't realize just how bad a clogged system was making them feel. I personally was bouncing off the walls. Others experience skin eruptions and boating. When a colonic is done, the fecal matter goes straight to the sewer system. No chemicals are involved, so this is considered an alternative method compared to conventional medicine. One colonic can be like taking away 30 bowel movements. Imagine that! Can you imagine how you feel afterwards? Once you remove this guk, allow your body to heal compared to right away ingesting more gook.

Hydrotherapy In General

External hydrotherapy comes in the form of a spa. If you join a gym or fitness center, you won't have to worry about waiting to go on vacation to get to a spa. Sure they have them in hotels, but how often do you go into a hotel? I joined La Fitness precisely for that. Of course, there were other incentives but that was one of the main ones. You come out relaxed every time. The jets in the water massage you. The temperature of the water has a therapeutic effect just as in olden days where people went inside hot springs.

Drinking Distiled Water

When you have kidney problems you are asked to drink distilled water. This is because doctors know that chlorinated water is heavy laden with chemicals, particularly fluoride and chlorine. Common sense will tell you that chlorine will destroy you. Look what it does to clothes. Chlorine in wine destroys you. The wine you drink now is not the same wine in Yeshua's time. Modern wine has chlorine too. KV recommended that I drink ozonated water. Some will say just add food grade hydrogen peroxide to it. Whatever the case, you will notice the difference between those and tap water. Ozonated water will give you more oxygen at the cellular level. Some methods are better than others. Whatever you do, don't rely on tap water. When your kidney is compromised, it does not need additional chemicals to process. It is really too much to ask it. It's like you're saying "I know you weren't created to process cadmium, lead and arsenic gobbledygook, but could you also process fluoride while you're at it?"

You see there are many different ways to get your body toxic. There is cellular toxicity, intestinal toxification, blood toxicity, heavy metal poisoning; and you have to address each issue. When your kidneys are in question, you are usually that far gone. Now you have to use glutathione to detoxify the body. Lack of amino acids depletes the glutathione level in the liver. You need vitamin C and selenium. Selenium is a detoxifier. Magnetic clay as a footbath pulls toxins out of your body because nerves at the end of the foot are connected to all organs of your body. Clay has negative charges and that is a good thing. Ever hear of the ionic footbath? If nothing else, drink plenty of water. Fruits have lots of water. If you cut down on fruits and don't drink water, you are stressing your kidneys. The kidney uses water to carry nutrients to the cell. The kidneys filter the blood in an attempt to remove toxins. Imagine what the kidney is thinking when you deprive it of water and fed it meat. She is thinking, "it's bad enough there are heavy metals in the shower water and air, now I have to process this without water?" Face it! It is too much to ask! Then you top it off with potato chips. Sometimes cheese is added. Others times macaroni in a hardened form is forced down the throat. When you get hiccups, your organs are really mad at you. They are boiling over with grief. And boy do they have a bone to pick with you. Can you blame them? These are soldiers, who don't complain much. For decades, they put up with your nonsense. The worst part is you don't even realize you are stressing them. We take our bodies for granted. We expect it to function regardless. Just remember, chocolate, and pound cakes have zero fiber. Digest that! Soon, the kidneys will come up with a movie called "Digest This!" Holy macaroni, why not just eat holy basil and be through with it. Holy basil is an anti-inflammatory. People do not realize that they are causing their own inflammation, by what they eat.

Water Retention Remedies

People with water retention problems should take parsley, celery and watermelon. Also helpful are vitamin B6, magnesium oxide, potassium citrate, Uva Ursi [found in the CKLS complex] corn silk and hydrangea. As far as laxatives go. I paid twice for my whistle. Cascara Sagrada appears in CKLS [$18.00]. I keep ginger root at home. Figs, prunes and dates are also indispensable. Figs and dates address stomach issues that are surprisingly pleasant. Though they taste good, they were designed to clear stomach problems. They're all part of the Mother Diet, and I grew up eating them. And by the way, they make you go to the bathroom. If nothing else will move you, figs and dates will! I don't know about you, but I had a constipation problem. So you see, it doesn't matter how healthy you ate in the past. It has already been proven that if you stray from a good diet, the bad results are almost immediate. Many people don't realize that the garlic and spices they put in meat is what's keeping them alive. Read up on any herb and spice and their medicinal properties and you will see what I mean. No wonder there were spice wars. I go to pharmacies and I see yucca and wild yame in pill form. My brother would say just eat the stuff. He can't understand people taking a bunch of pills. Now, there are many liquid options for people who don't like taking pills.

One supplement I took had African pygeum in it. It is touted as anti-inflammatory and addressing urinary health. But there were other herbs in the mix. The best thing to do is to read each herb to make sure they don't cancel each other. That is why it is always good to consult with a professional nutritionist. Many times scientists disagree with what herbs do because sometimes these experiments are done on animals under very specific circumstances that are questionable. But not all studies are questionable.

People think it is normal to go to the bathroom once a week. You should go several times a day. Apples are emphasized for people with constipation. They even had the nerve to include tamarind as part of a laxative complex. In my country tamarind is part of the diet. You either eat it as is, or in a drink form, or as a sauce for meat. Face it; don't turn your nose up at things that keep you regular. You'll appreciate it one day when your body shuts down like mine did. My body stopped digesting to the point where I would throw up as soon as I would eat. So after paying twice for the same ingredient, the lesson I learned is, stick to your original diet if it works. The Latin diet is very rich in fiber. Yucca, yautia, name [nyame], and coconut all have fiber to boot. Africans eat a lot of these same items.

Avoid Cigarette Smoke

Being exposed to smoke can make you toxic. That is because smoke has cadmium, tar, cyanide, arsenic, lead, nicotine, and other things that are bad for you. Not only do smokers shorten their lives, but also they shorten the lives of others by putting these chemicals into the air. The original Indians who smoked did not put chemicals into their tobacco. This is the basis of the lawsuit. What we do affect others, whether it is smoking or eating a bad diet. The germs you carry as you decay, affect other people's health. Your smell is toxic to others. It puts them in a bad mood. Bad mood is bad for health and so on. This is the basis for my "My Body Is My Temple" organization. Someone came up with a similar name later and I never did process the name. But I still have the business card.

Avoid Radiation

We are exposed to radiation to a larger degree than we think. What happens to these rays that are led into the environment. Do you think they just disappear into thin air? Nothing disappears, just as I stated in my poem called "The Planet And The Soul." It is not just machines that emit radiation. The earth itself emits radiation in certain areas. We used to use female technology back in the days of Atlantis and Lemuria in its early stage before the downfall. We used the stick for dowsing and so on. We were able to gage whether too much radiation was being emitted in certain parts of the earth. When Ibrahiym [Abraham, Brahma], and Moses and all the people of God were being guided or being told to move or where to live, part of the reasoning had to do with certain areas being heavily radiated. You couldn't just live anywhere. Now thanks to modernity we have wires hanging above us, below us, that emit dangerous levels of radiation. Add cellular phones, microwaves, television radiation and you have unpredictable results. We hear of the dangers of cellular phones and it's association with brain tumors. Same with microwave and computers. But did you know you could reverse this with the tourmaline stone? You can also use cedar. Next time you're on the computer, use the stone of the sun. Let's not take our life for granted. Our mission here on Earth has not been accomplished. Why were you born? Do you know? Are there secret societies preventing you from accomplishing your mission? Does the Devil do everything in its power to tempt you? Why was the Bible written? What's behind all the mysteries? According to Adamah, the purpose of the game called life is to get out alive. The Devils puts things in your path to prevent you from accomplishing your mission. It's as simple as that. When you learn a life giving technique, help a sister out or a brother.

For a chemical free shampoo try using clay. Clay draws the toxins out of your scalp. It also draws out radiation. You may have to oil your scalp with natural moisturizers such as shae butter after drying clay. There are many beauty products out there that destroy you without you even giving it as much as a second thought. If you don't make it yourself you won't know what's in it. I make my own beauty products, or health enhancers, whether it be lipsticks, foundation etc. Some of the ingredients in commercial products will destroy you. You will be shocked at what's in it.

Chelation

Another way to detoxify the body is through a process called chelation. This procedure removes heavy metals from your system. Chelating reverses the ill effects of pesticides, herbicides, lead, mercury, cadmium, arsenic, plastics and other pollutants. Chelating acts as a free radical scavenger. But if you find chelating to be expensive, you can find a cheap way to do it yourself. Certain herbs and roots naturally chelate cells. Selenium is one such item. You can ingest charcoal to fight cancerous cells and to get rid of poison in your system. When you ingest poison the medical doctors will give you charcoal. You see, they are utilizing secrets that have been known for years to indigenous peoples. Fermentation of sugar causes oxygen to disappear. Lack of oxygen causes cancer. Now you see why they say sugar is the enemy. Cancer cells love fermentation.

In fact, cell mutation came about as a result of lack of oxygen. You see, PH level has a relationship with oxygen. Try eating meat and zero vegetables and see what happens to you over time. You grow moles. Moles manifest due to a lack of oxygen. But that is not all. The outside growths are just what erupt. But what is brewing on the inside is even worst. What's brewing inside could be cancer, heat disease, kidney disease, diabetes and so on. Try mustard seed and Ashwaganda to reverse this situation of lack of oxygen. You can also try food grade hydrogen peroxide but you must follow instructions well or else. Try anything green and raw in order to increase oxygen in your body. Volcanic minerals get rid of cancerous cells as well.

Oregano

Want to get rid of bacteria in your body? Tired of having colds and want to eliminate the root cause - bacteria and food rotting inside you. Try real oregano [real not commercialized please], try garlic and onions. Also try fulvic acid. Humic Fulvic Acid will improve your DNA. How it does this, is by eliminating toxins that you get from vaccinations, food and all the other methods we mentioned earlier such as water, air etc. They are the smallest molecules on the planet, so it acts on the cellular level. It has been said that it is the link between organic and inorganic states. Some say it is DNA from other lifetimes and call it Mother's Milk. Some people forget that we get toxins from drugs. Let's not forget over-the-counter drugs. Modern peoples are literally bombarded with toxins. There is no escaping it. The idea behind self cleanse is to bring back the ph balance while getting rid of heavy metals. That is not easy, but it can be done. Many people have done it. But it is kept very quiet. Once you find out disease is irreversible, self-healing is a snap. The Indians used it. Shop at the international stores and automatically; you'll see the difference in these products.

They're also cheaper in the international stores and farmer's markets. You'll notice the aroma is different; and how the product works. There are no caked up preservatives or pesticides. And you wonder why other cultures live longer.

DNA Repair

Capitalistic greed can kill societies. Greed can take lives. The Black Indians educated the red Indians, and they have been using fulvic acid since. It repairs DNA. Red Indians are a mixture of Whites and Blacks. Let's get real. Some people refuse to acknowledge the similarity in cultures of the Africans and Indians. Some go as far as to say there is no connection between the Mounds, and pyramids of Western or Eastern peoples. They prefer to hide behind words like coincidences. The point here is that no one wants to acknowledge the African contribution to society. They want everyone to believe in the inferiority of Africans. Thus they depict Africans on TV as inferior beings. You never see modern African cities, though they exist. The best thing for people to do is visit for themselves. The African contribution must be emphasized because the African approach is holistic. Europeans treat inflammation separate from other conditions. They are confused as to the root causes of disease. What should be done is to treat the whole individual rather than treating part of the individual. When you go shopping at health food stores, the products will say, "this product has not been evaluated by the food and drug administration." Just be glad it hasn't. The Food And Drug Administration is not your friend. If they try to shut down health food stores and products with zero harmful effect, they are not your friends. A product called Master Detox "Mother's Milk" is something I tried. It promises to energize, oxygenates and chelate. For people with kidney problems, those are the results you want. This product is on the expensive level $36.00. One way to look at it is "am I worth it?" People may or may not notice the difference. People have different levels of toxicity. But one thing is for sure, whether you use red clay or bentonite clay, toxins will be removed. So, never forget the power of mother earth. Clay is the cheap way to go if you are strapped for cash. Regardless how you got kidney disease, you have toxins and need to detoxify. This is because the kidneys are the filters of the blood. The kidneys are where toxins accumulate. They can accumulate in the spleen and liver too. Some people get cancer in the liver and spleen, after bouts with kidney so don't take it lightly. Watch out for stomach cancer, pancreatic cancer and other complications. Remember also that green things have chlorophyll and they also purify the blood. When you go into dialysis, it is an attempt by doctors to purify your blood. You can use St John's Wort, red clover, and sorrel to purify the blood. These natural products have zero side effects compared to dialysis.

The Ugly Truth About Dialysis

The ugly truth about dialysis is that it is costly number one. Number two, it takes a long time to recuperate from it - four days. Furthermore, you don't need a license to operate a dialysis clinic. The results are minimal compared to natural products and you still die. Sorry, but I had to get that truth out. I realize certain industries won't like me. Maybe they imagine they will lose money. But I just want what is in the best interest of people. This is what I tried. These are the results of my findings. People are dying by the droves. Somebody has to care. Never before have so many people been plagued with disease at such level. Why do we close our eyes at the statistics? We don't even have to be statistician to see what's going on. Everyone knows people used to live longer, not only in Biblical times, but just as recently as the last century! People know that heart attacks and cancer were unusual diseases. Now they're as common as a dime. It is time we each become saviors of each other and the Earth. This destructive pattern is very unnatural. If you suspect there is something wrong e-mail me or write me at mercy123123@aol.com. I want to hear your stories. There are people that feel very bad because they sense something is terribly wrong. Remember, there is strength in numbers. Please tell me I am not alone. I do not want to see the Earth destroyed. But we each can make a difference. Let us save planet Earth for the sake of future posterity.

Take a Wholistic Approach

One of the people who took the holistic approach was Dr. Llaila Africa. He feels that there is no reason to change nature that has provided us with everything we need. Read his books and you'll learn all about the holistic [wholeness] approach, which has been embraced by Africa since time untold. The community model is emphasized because there is strength in numbers. We can do more - together. An individual alone can become overwhelmed trying to save the world by himself. But if others join or pitch in, you will not feel so alone. Sharing resources is a must. Whatever your mission is, get others to join you so you won't be so stressed. Stress can kill. It is the basis of many diseases. He also points out the importance of minerals and amino acids. Now everyone is jumping on the bandwagon. Our people are astonishing.

Eating foods from a depleted soil can be useless. You're not getting the vitamins, minerals and trace elements you were meant to get. Not rotating crops or burnings can leave you hanging. Raping the land as some call it can devastate your health. Please read my poem called "Health Consciousness" for inspiration. The spirit will come in you and say, "let's make a change." Prayer also works. If you are trying to heal, there is nothing like faith. As some say "don't claim it [bad health]. That's what I did and it has carried me so far; much further than others who started out sick with me. I don't claim to be a doctor, but I can say I have avoided dialysis so far. And I enjoy a better quality of life than the others because of my lifestyle change. I am not saying I am perfect. I could have made the change more drastic if I really wanted to heal quicker. Due to force of habit it went a lot slower than it should have. I am here to say, if you love life embrace it enough to change your lifestyle. If you must do it gradually then so be it. But do not continue on the same path and expect change. Don't eat scavengers and expect God to take care of it. That's like mocking God. God clearly states do not eat fish with shells, fish weighing certain pounds, animals with cloven hoof /do not chew the cud and so on. When you study these animals [what not to eat] you learn that they are the scavengers of the earth. You learn that they give you high cholesterol. You learn that they eat anything, including heavy metals that pollute the waters. Their purpose is to clean the bottom of the ocean. Once you begin to eat crabs, clams, and catfish, you place your kidney in a strange situation. You are asking your kidney to process cadmium, arsenic, lead, mercury and radiation as if your body was created to be a scavenger, which it wasn't. You try to digest foods that animals with two stomachs were created for. Yet you expect to be healthy. That's like quitting your job and expecting money to fall out the sky "because God will provide." That's like saying, "let's not ever do anything because the future has already been orchestrated." It doesn't work like that. There are no free rides. In that case, why did the elders, and prophets and the Son of God give us parables about the talents -how talents are used and underused and the dire consequence. Did He not call his servant lazy? We are here to serve a higher force. We are stewards. In other words, we were entrusted with the earth, but if we pollute it and poison the population, are we then not bad stewards? The earth is not here to be an amusement for you to do what you please with it, while killing species. Every action has a consequence. The sooner you learn how we are interdependent the better. All species of life forms are here for a reason. You eliminate one and the whole eco-system suffers.

Nutritional Counseling

If your body is depleted you can put nutrition back into your body by drinking or eating the following; Irish moss, bee pollen, sea vegetables, especially bladder wrack. I used bladder wrack to keep my high blood pressure in check. Then, I went into nutritional counseling with sister Adamah. she taught me to use the ph paper and can do the same for you and so much more. Her information can be found in the appendix. Listening to motivational tapes came in handy as well. The sister provided me with motivational tapes and DVD's that bombard you with useful information.

Some say our grandparents ate junk. Keep in mind that was the first generations of junk food eaters. How many potato chips does it take to affect your health? Forty-eight or 2,000? We don't know, but we push the body to the limit, just as children try their parent's patience to see how far they can go. Our forefathers didn't have to deal with the level of electromagnetic radiation that we do today. Nor did they deal with the same amount of stress, pesticides, preservatives and so on. Do not drink sodas just because your folks did. How long have sodas been around compared to how long the earth has been around? My point exactly. Our fore-parents were not exposed to manmade chemicals as we are now. We are facing artificial heat, and artificial light. Some of you recall the kerosene lantern/lamp. It really wasn't that long ago. If you are in tune with your body, you will notice a zap in energy as you experience artificial light and artificial heat. Try staying in bed under artificial heat radiator for a week, right at your bedside. Leave the television on constantly while you are at it and what do you notice? Anyone who works with computers know the drainage I am referring to. It's no different with television and microwaves. I said stay in bed because there are people who have the flu stay in bed and after a while they realize they can only watch but so much television. One week will do it, if not less.

Sweat More with Saunas

Today we treat sweat as though it is unnatural. This may just be part of our tragic fall. People from other epochs used to sweat a lot due to weather conditions and more time being outdoors. They also walked a lot more than we do. The advantage for them is that toxins came out of their bodies through sweat. The same can be said for hot countries where air conditioning is "new" or minimal. We do not sweat any more. Air conditioners will not allow it. Our homes, offices and cars are air-conditioned. We spend all day going from artificial weather to another. What happens when we don't sweat? Toxins do not exude out of your bodies. People nowadays drive even to the grocery stores. If you join a fitness club, you can take advantage of the sweat lodge. At least that is what it was called in Indian times. Today people call it a sauna. The Indians used herbs to add aromatherapy to the experience. Be creative. Steam some heat in your bathroom and burn resins such as sage, which is very cleansing.

Joining a fitness club is worth it just for the sauna alone. Otherwise be creative and build one of your own.

Walk, Relax and Be Merry

Part of the reason people walk less is the way communities are being built. Unless you live in New York, DC or some other inner city, you probably drive to the grocery stores. Now ask yourself how people got to the general stores before the invention of modern cars. They walked! Walking also helps you to lose weight. It gets the metabolism going. Manual labor was en vogue when it came to cutting wood, washing clothes, working in a farm etc. Some people are glad those days are over, but they are paying with their lives for being couch potatoes. Some people think exercising is a pain in the neck. But I say have fun while you exercise. Why not try dancing? It's fun. Put on a Latin CD or an Afrikan CD and if you're not dancing you're not human. Enjoy life. All work and no play make Jack a dull boy. But they forgot to say it also makes him sick. What I did was to join La Fitness for a free week. I liked it so much I accepted regular membership. Try it; you might just like it enough to sign up. I was like a kid in a candy store. I tried the bicycle, the treadmill, and the arm muscle machine. The tummy machines were my favorite. They even have hip-hop classes! That was my favorite class. But don't get carried away and do too much too soon. You wouldn't want to drive up your blood pressure. But if you do, just eat some garlic and relax. They have a smoothie bar there, by the way. Did I mention they have a spa and swimming pool? The hot tub releases stress, relaxes muscles and hydrotherapy goes to work. They also have equipment weighing practically nothing that you can take inside the water. But once you take them inside the water you can feel the resistance, so it's a form of exercise while having fun.

My favorite was the sauna. Ladies and gentlemen, we do not sweat enough. Think about it, we have air conditioner at home, we hop into cars with air conditioners, and we work at offices with air conditioning. Do we ever sweat? No! That's why we're so sick. It's not so much that we no longer work in farms. Even the Indians and Egyptians utilized saunas. To the Western Indians, it was known as sweat lodges, where sage was used to create scents while sweating. Could it get any better? The Indians sure knew what they were doing. By now it should be apparent that sweating is a necessary part of life. Not sweating causes the bodily toxins to stay inside the body, whereas they belong outside the body. You don't have to stay in the sauna a long while. It is your effort that counts.

Get Plenty of Rest

There are those who wonder about how much rest one should get. According to one source nine hours. The body is supposed to be at rest by 10:00. Boy did my mother raise me right! There was no talking after 10:00. Studies have shown that REM sleep begins at ten o'clock at night. Without REM sleep you are not healthy or rejuvenated. Your body is supposed to sleep in total darkness; otherwise you get no real rest. In the city [and suburbs] you get light from the light poles. No matter how much you shut your blinds [or curtains] some light always sneaks in. And we wonder why we are sick. In order for the body to completely recharge itself, there has to be total darkness.

Do Not Expose Self to Death Rays

If you have ever experienced chemotherapy, you have been exposed to an unacceptable level of toxicity. Sometimes the cure can kill you when you're talking about modern methods of curing. As I observed this and how tired people are after dialysis [four days to recuperate], I told myself I would not subject myself to these barbaric treatments. There has to be another way. I would rather die than be killed unnecessarily by some machine or people who may not know what they are doing.

Minimize Bacteria

After I did the colonic I drank tea tree oil. Tea tree oil will get rid of bacteria. It is very strong so you have to use it sparingly. I know it kills bacteria, even strep throat. But I was trying to kill the bacteria in my stomach and bladder. Garlic also kills bacteria. My daughter didn't like garlic or onions - to our detriment. I didn't know the power of garlic and onions at that time. Onions and garlic lower blood pressure. Red onionskin has quercetine. People use this substance in medicine to cure kidney conditions. My brother Lorenzo would say why not just eat the stuff? He thinks capitalists are just out to make a profit. One thing is for sure. The rulers of the Earth right now have created a false impression of lack in order to create fear into buying their products. It doesn't matter to them how many people die or suffer in the process- all in the name of profit. If you purchase medicinal herbs, barks, roots and plants from the bulk bins at the co-ops/health food stores, you'll save a lot of money and grief. They allow you to buy small amounts at a time - just enough to cure yourself.

Eating bitters will assist in your healing. Parasites hate bitters. They thrive off putrefication and fermentation. But once you eat bitters, see how quickly they disappear. Evacuations will not be a problem. After watching someone lose weight this way I was inspired to try the same. She became a "girl" all over again.

Now I'm more mature and want to live so I cut sugar out. If I want to sweeten something now I use Agave syrup, which is natural and has a higher glycemic index. This means it's safe for diabetics.

Many people come to me for help at work because they see that I eat different and am basically a health nut in their eyes. Boni asked, "What do you recommend for energy?" I replied, "Bee pollen because it has everything the body needs." She's thinking it is the same substance that causes allergens in the trees and rejected it. I don't argue with people. I replied, "Try a shake with mango, and kelp. You came to me for help." There is something magical about this formula. Kelp is a source of calcium. I don't take pills from stores including health food stores. Calcium supplements have a lot of fillers. In fact, there is a correlation between kidney dysfunction and calcium so do your homework in getting the most natural source of calcium.

I take pumpkin seeds to kill parasites. Also, I eat coconut. After 72 hours, parasites disappear from the colon of those who eat coconut. Coconut is an under-appreciated miracle food.

Real Cranbebby for the Bladder

The saying that cranberry juice helps with urinary tract problems is an understatement. It doesn't hurt to drink cherry juice and blueberry juice either. I take magnesium for the bladder also. The most effective cranberry juice has no sugar and can be purchase in concentrated form from the health food store. During a most painful bladder infection, I drank this juice intermittent with garlic and oregano until the pain went away. I was not playing. It wasn't even about the taste at this point. It was that serious. The good news is it worked!

Strive to Alkalinize Your Body

If acidic foods keep the body unhealthy and disease cannot exist in an alkaline body, then the goal should be to alkalinize the body. All minerals alkalinize the body. Avoid meat. It is acidic. So are grains, sugar and soda. Fruits and vegetables alkalinize the body.

When the body becomes acidic the body deposits toxins to try to make the body more alkaline. This makes the body more acidic, so it's a vicious cycle. If you are in tune with your body you notice differing bodily reactions to different foods. You either feel energized or drained. If you feel sleepy after you eat, perhaps you are taxing your body with loads of digestive instructions. If you feel pain when you ingest sugar, that is your body's way of letting you know something is wrong. If you continue ingesting sugar, you are ignoring your body's signal. The respiratory enzymes are harmed and this harms your DNA. When acidic waste builds up, degenerative disease occurs. To protect your DNA from mutation, you need to watch you PH level. Meat, white flour, table salt and white sugar will alter your DNA. They initiate the aging process.

Reduce Acidity

Reishi mushrooms reduce the acidity of coffee. E. excell sells a product that contains Reishi mushrooms that tastes just like coffee. I used to put the pack in soymilk and it tasted better than a cappuccino! They also produce a great bee pollen product called concenergy. This product never let me down whenever my energy was depleted. It is designed to address nutrition solutions at the cellular level.

Germanium increases oxygen. When it comes to Reishi mushrooms and germanium, you can expect weight control and toxin removal. MSM alkalinizes. I took it for carpal tunnel and I got rid of my carpal tunnel forever. MSM creates oxygen and detoxifies. Whatever the case, I love it for removing my carpal tunnel for days on end. It wasn't just carpal tunnel that it addressed. I had shoulder pain, tennis elbow, and neck pain from being in the same position day in and day out doing repetitive work. The agency was not about to compensate me for any of my ills, so I had to find a cheap way to heal. Whether MSM is the essence of plants or dew or the sun I couldn't say. But whatever it is, it worked for me and it's natural. You get more nutrients in and more toxins out. The sulphur in MSM fights cancer. You can get MSM from the top of plants.

Blue green algae are another super-food. But it is special because it rids the body of radiation, heavy metals, and it alkalinizes. You should consider detoxifying with blue green algae because conventional treatments make the body more acidic. Cells cannot communicate with each other in an acidic state.

Reduce Inflamation

People with kidney problems have inflammation issues. Inflammation is a warning sign by the body that toxins are out of control and or that water retention is taking place. Some people's faces swell, when they eat too much sugar. For other people, it is salt. A great anti-inflammatory agent is aloe vera. It normalizes blood sugar just as cinnamon does. Other diuretics are celery seed, celery period and parsley. Eating too much animal protein can cause edema.

Do the Opposite of What Society Does

Most of my healing came from the kitchen - inexpensive remedies you find around the house. But I took it a step further, using, clay internally and externally, deep tissue massage, sauna, swimming, spa hydrotherapy, nutritional counseling. Basically everything that I preach about in my poems, I practiced. One thing that was not cheap was the Himalayan / miracle salt. It costs twenty-one dollars, but you get a lot. Not only that but think of what it does. Think of all the trace elements your body is missing and how most diseases can be attributed to trace element or mineral deficiency. Life

Essentials and Sevananda carries it. This means most co-ops should carry it if they are health conscious.

Let's talk about the false truth about salt and the real truth about salt. True or false - salt causes hypertension. Myth or truth; if you have kidney malfunction you have no business eating salt. My answer to both is, it depends on which salt, table salt or miracle [Himalayan] salt. I believed all this until I came across someone who healed her hypertension with salt. She said doctors would have you believing salty things don't heal. What she did was heal herself with seaweed, which is the saltiest thing you will ever taste. When you think about it, it makes sense. The ocean has always healed us. For those of you who don't know, it is well known in the Latin Community and Africa that the ocean has a healing powers. This particular individual used brown seaweed. She is no longer dependent on pharmaceuticals. Threw them away. She has never looked back.

As far as kidney issue, it would do you well to take miracle salt/Himalayan salt. Himalayan salt has 72 trace elements.

Table salt is essentially a poison because in the process minerals have been removed. Iodine is then added back into the mix. Studies have shown that isolated chemicals added on as vitamins do not benefit the body. As I said earlier isolation of vitamins is never a good idea. The makers of supplements miss the point of the synergistic way that nutrients interact with your body.

Himalayan salt is unprocessed and thus does not act as a poison to the system. People used to venerate salt because in those days it was not processed, thus you could appreciate all of its benefits. Did you know your sinus clear when you take salt in its pristine form? In other words, you get rid of mucous and obtain all the benefits of its trace elements and minerals. It is recommended that you add a little rock of salt to an eight ounce glass of water. Follow the instructions on the label and you will testify of your own that ancient knowledge was on time.

Avoid Table Salt

Table salt's connection to kidney disease and hypertension is well known. Furthermore, people's own experiences confirm the correlation. But when we study the history of salt, a whole new picture emerges. In antiquity salt was more valuable than gold. Why do you think that is? You see, people valued their health. They knew all the money in the world could not buy health. That is, unless you were following Hippocrate's words "let your food be your medicine." In Latin America the word for salt is sal. There, you can see where the word salary has a root that means salt. That's because you were paid in salt not money. Pristine salt has all the trace minerals the body needs. You could not survive without salt. In fact, some of today's diseases or mutations go back in time when some people were deprived access to salt or it was unavailable. People in the Caucus Mountains were particularly deprived. Today they are paying for it with a condition that bears witness to the importance of melanin. Many people now take melanin for sleep and other reasons. You see, it is all related. The root cause of most diseases is mineral deficiency. This is why many people built their cities near large bodies of water. Salt comes from the sea. The sea has all the minerals the body needs. Salt is dried up sea. Go bathe in any ocean before noon and you will heal. The body is composed of salt and water. Originally all life formed in the sea. To this day infants swim in a sea of salty water just as in the beginning.

In a vision/revelation I am asked by the elder [one of the 24 elders], "What is the chemical composition of salt?" That left a deep impression on me. It was not an optional test question. I heard the voice clear as day. It was a question that had to be answered as soon as possible. That's when my real search on salt began. I believe they were trying to tell me there is a difference between table salt and real salt. Not only that but when you research you educate and heal at the same time.

Azafran

I treated high blood pressure with a combination of the following. Brown algae, olive leaf, and sassafras. Azafran is the Latin name for sassafras. It is expensive, but worth it- all twelve dollars. It has a peppery taste. Azafran helps with circulation. This was one of the Egyptian's favorite herbs. The Moors brought this herb to Spain.

The curanderos used it for cancer. It is excellent for kidneys and liver. This herb also helps the heart. See an herbologist for the recommended amount. We complain that some things are expensive, but it's all relative. Would you rather pay thousands of dollars for a heart transplant or twelve dollars for a pack of azafran? You already know what I will say.

Sassafras can be found in Arabian, Indian, African or Latin stores. But you will also find it in the spice section of any American store. When doctors want to reduce your cholesterol, they inject you with "crocetina," a chemical that comes from azafran. Keep in mind that Latin Americans, people from Spain, as well as people from the Caribbean Islands and Africans use azafran freely to season their foods. They also have fewer heart attacks than those who don't. So, paying a little bit more is sometimes worth it. Azafran (sassafras) gives oxygen, thus preventing blood clots. It has also proven to prevent high blood pressure. The knowledge our ancestors have is amazing. I am telling you this because I not only researched it, but I had good results with it.

In a world that is supposed to be so modern, people sure are sick. Everyone I spoke to knows someone who is affected by diabetes or kidney troubles. People's faces swell up and they are clueless. Sometimes it's just the eyes. Sometimes it is the ankles. More people than ever are having urinary problems. Kidney failure leads to death. Do not be fooled by mild symptoms.

Everyone should take the supplements in this book because kidney inflammation, show no symptoms, but everyone is exposed to chemicals. I had it and didn't even know it. Almost died, but I am a strong woman. I knew I was not finished with my mission, so I had to do whatever it took to survive. I had to crawl out of bed though severely infirmed. If something happens to me now I would feel better because my book is out. If they kill me because of this book the sales will hit through the roof.

Edema Treatment

I ate celery sticks and celery juice to reduce my edema/water retention. This is considered a diuretic. I would also purchase a readymade combination of celery juice, lemons and cucumber.

Thus, I not only got rid of my water retention problem, but I also made my body more alkaline! Burdock is also a diuretic and reportedly excellent for renal problems, and painful urination. The plant called bucchu was used in South Africa long before the Europeans came. It was used for urinary problems due to antiseptic oil within the plant. Bucchu also helps with water retention. Today doctors use it to alleviate bloating during pre-menstrual syndrome, which essentially comes from water retention. Once again, herbs come to the rescue. There is a relationship between high blood pressure and water retention. You may use Bucchu in the form of a tincture [half a teaspoon] that can be bought from health food stores. Otherwise you may use a tea from your local co-op.

When we go to the hospital, we are intravenously fed salt and water. What could have been the start of this tradition? Could it be that the original salt had all its minerals and thus we got our minerals originally from salt and water? No matter what your problem is, by the time the salt and water is injected in you, suddenly you feel better. You even breathe better. The doctor smiles a knowing smile as he announces that you were dehydrated (prior to the IV). You go home while wondering why your salt doesn't do that. The next time you visit the ER you see the word "Sodium Chloride" written in big bold letters. Then you wonder, "Am I missing something?" Well guess what? The doctors know table salt will not cure you. But they don't tell you stop eating it altogether. They tell you to cut down on it. The same with meat, "cut your protein intake." What you are missing concerning the sodium chloride is that doctors use food grade hydrogen peroxide in the IV and no they do not use table salt. Don't even think about asking them for the secret. They're not in the business of telling. I hope they don't hate me for this but I have to save people. Too many people are checking out unnecessarily.

If they are using table salt or a laboratory created salt, then obviously they are adding electrolytes and possibly minerals. Whatever the case, it is time we took a closer look at salt - real salt. People are afraid to overdose on salt and rightly so. We hear stories about hypertension being caused by salt. When people suffer with edema or water retention, the first thing the doctor says is cut down on salt. Yet, in the ancient days salt was so highly priced, people were paid in salt in place of gold. How powerful is that? The word salary comes from salt. In Spanish "sal" means salt. There are many other telling etymology stemming from the word salt, which tends to paint a picture of just how highly valued this rock was. Yes, the original salt has a rock like formation. As a matter of fact, the best salt is a pink looking rock coming from the Himalayas. Many people will tell you that sea salt sold in health food stores are a good substitute for table salt. But what many people don't know is that there are many varieties of sea salt. Though it comes from the health food store, it may still be processed. The perfect example is green and white Stevia. Stevia, the sugar substitute made from a plant with a natural sweet taste is green in its natural form. At health food stores it is white. At coops, it is green. So it's always good to buy herbs, roots, and alternative medicine products from coops since they offer bulk buying in its pristine state. Salt also has different colorations. Some people swear by the gray salt, Celtic salt and black salt. I have tried them all. Gray salt or Celtic salt is better than the white sea salt. But the best of all by far is the miracle salt, also known as Himalayan salt. Let me tell you a secret. Anything that grows or is produced in the Himalayas is good for you. You should always look at how long people live in certain areas. Is it the pure mountain air? Is it the soil, which has not been raped or abused? It's both. But don't just take my word for it. Know that of all people who have tried all these products, none of them have a single complaint about Himalayan pink salt or miracle salt. The name miracle should be a clue. That is no exaggeration. This is the only salt that you cannot overdose on. Ask yourself why. The answer is all the minerals are still intact. It has not been perverted. Salt in its natural state provides everything the body needs. Why do you think people fought and died for salt? The same is true of Stevia – wars were fought over it. Now table salt has been robbed off its nutrients. As long as people take away from the whole, of a nature made products, there will be problems. This is very valuable information. Table salt kills. It is a poison and should be thrown away. Mother nature was not intended to operate in a vacuum. Mad scientists, I mean, modern scientists have no idea how "ingredients" in nature operate together. The same thing occurs with wheat. Rob wheat off its wheat germ and fiber and you have a sure recipe for constipation, death and diabetes, clogged arteries, and the list is endless. Anyone who partakes off these non-foods posing as foods is really asking for it. Himalayan rock salt (pink) is like a lump of minerals and trace elements.

The proportion of the 72 elements found in miracle salt closely resembles human blood in its healthiest form. So that when you go in the hospital, they are trying to replace your bad blood with plasma they call Sodium Chloride. Trade secrets. Ever wonder why they don't feed you instead? We are made up of 70% water. The salt carries the minerals throughout the blood. That is, if we are speaking of pure salt. It makes you look at salt in a whole new way. So, not surprisingly some people have cured their hypertension with, of all things, salt! For example, smart people use brown seaweed to cure their condition of high blood pressure. There are angry people out there who feel betrayed by the medical profession, who have people addicted to lab chemicals. Taking advantage of sick people or thriving off of them is not a pretty picture. There are always doctors who are good or simply were not taught any better. So when I wrote the poem "Health Consciousness," I had the predators in mind.

You know how doctors give you a saline solution for everything from serious chronic disorders, to mouth rinse? Well, now, you can make your own saline solution, except you'll be using real salt. You can rinse your nose with it, drink it or gargle with it. I mostly drink it and cook with it. It is very precious to me.

If you have high blood pressure, I suggest you control it with brown seaweed, because having high blood pressure for a long time can mess up your kidneys. In addition, you should replace table salt with miracle salt. Some people with these problems eliminate salt altogether from the diet. Eliminating table salt is a good thing. But don't forget that natural blood is salty. Don't forget that your body needs real salt. Don't forget your minerals. And do not rely on one source to get all your minerals. Supplement your diet with bee pollen. Bee pollen has all the vitamins and minerals the body will ever need. Also eat in proportions according to the make-up of the human body. The percentage of boron found on the earth is a good indicator of how much boron you should take in proportion to your body. The percentage of copper found on earth is the same proportion found in a healthy body. We are children of the earth and the secret to getting out alive is to imitate the earth. Eating the wrong proportion is the problem. That's why you hear that chaparral is bad for the liver yet good. You also hear that depending on whom you talk to, certain things are bad for the kidneys yet good. Instead of being confused, study the earth's minerals in proportion to itself and you. That's how you should eat.

Some people may pity me saying, "that's right, you can't eat salt." Little do they know. I am also pleased to announce that one of my favorite snacks is flat seaweed that is crunchy. It eats like potato chips and does not harm your health [once you have brought your blood pressure under control]. This is the same thing used for wrapping sushi called Nori. Isn't it wonderful that now we have salt substitutes to satisfy the potato chip craving? The very fact that we crave salt means there is something in salt that the body needs. The body is craving minerals – specifically iodine, calcium and real sodium. Nori has iron and calcium. I am proud to announce that my blood pressure is under control now that I changed my lifestyle.

Eat food as it is and quit tampering with it. And then there are those things that you have to acquire a taste for.

Avoid Dairy Products & Meat

One thing is for sure; no one should be eating dairy products if they have kidney problems. Nor should they eat meat. Too much protein can kill the kidneys. Certain people are especially susceptible and vulnerable. Infants are said to become ill as adults if fed cow's formula. If mucous is the root cause of all disease, then why would anyone ingest dairy products? The more in tune you become with your body, the more you'll notice how certain foods make you feel. When you eat, you either feel depleted or energized. You'll also notice that the smells are horrific. But we close our eyes and eat it because the lobbyists who write the textbooks have convinced teachers to teach your children about the pyramid food lie. I can only feel sorry for people who have never been exposed to anything else. The author of New Choices In Natural Healing has linked diabetes type II [insulin dependent] to an infant formula using cow's milk. They also suggest that the reason pills don't provide vitamins as fruits and vegetables do is because of the micronutrients, and phytochemicals found in these natural products. These micronutrients were designed to protect plants against insects. I've following Dr Llaila Africa's teachings but I had to throw in a white person for those skeptics that need the white man's approval. Dr Llaila Africa also suggests the same. In Africa the philosophy is that the whole is better than its separate parts. But the pale man tradition suggests the opposite in a very contrasting way. This is what I had in mind when I wrote He Loves To Separate. Then I went on to say, "he thinks by separating, he'll get to know a thing." Now if it were up to me, I would say no one should eat meat. The poisons from dead carcasses putrefying causes skin eruptions. These eruptions are well described in the Bible, the chapter called Deuteronomy. So why add poison on top of poison? Meat eaters who love their lifestyles will argue with me on this one. I say read Deuteronomy again for clarification. And while you're at it, read the other scrolls. What did John the Baptist eat? Was he not fortified of God? Did he not have visions after a vegetarian diet? That is my point exactly. If you want to be holy [whole -ly] then you must follow the lifestyle of those before you. People who excavate mummies know what I'm talking about. Some mummies have been discovered with bee-pollen still inside them. This is a clue as to what our ancestors ate. Many people are not aware that bee pollen has all the nutrition that the body needs.

Look at your teeth and how they are shaped, and that should tell you how much meat you should eat, if at all. I say everyone stay away from meat. Anything more than that is an addiction. Some of us were forced into eating meat when it is wrong for our body types. Schools stress eating dairy and meat, but we found out later it was politics. If your teeth are small and straight, you should be a vegetarian. What makes a person white or black is not the color of the skin. Anthropologists hold that it is the teeth that make people the race that they are. Black people tend to have small straight teeth. This is why they have such a hard time with protein. Many are also lactose intolerant. Whites tend to be protein deficiency quicker than any other race. their teeth are usually bigger, and longer. Why people do not eat for their blood type is probably due to all the race mixing and adopting other people's cultures. If you have teeth that are clearly not made to eat vegetables then goat meat is the best meat there is. I agree with the author of the biblical diet in that sense. If your teeth were made for vegetables you'll know it because you'll have straight teeth and small. The opposite would be true if you were made to eat meat. Your teeth would tend to be longer, sharper, and your gums would not show as much. Real Blacks who have not been mixed have the features of vegetarians. But now that you know, it should be easy to understand why you are having so many problems. As a child I had a real hard time accepting meat. My body instinctively knew it wasn't meant to be. My instincts also told me killing wasn't right. As we get older, we get desensitized through acculturation. More power to you if you have the teeth for it. But I had to be forced fed. My sister thought it was an attention getter to battle with Mom at the dinner table. But I actually was not only repelled at the thought of killing another life just so I could eat, but I literally could not chew it let alone digest it. I found out later that it takes about four hours to digest meat. The Koyfman Center in Norcross Georgia where I get my colonics has confirmed it. The scary thing is that some people actually believe they cannot get protein except through meat. People have really been brainwashed. Hemp seed and other seeds, beans, nuts, some vegetables, some fruits [avocado is sometimes considered a vegetable and sometimes considered a fruit] and ginger have protein. When I realized my digestion problem was out of control, I began to eat pineapples papayas [lechosa] and ginger. All are good for digestion. For the pain I take willow bark, cherry bark, oak bark, and blackberries. In Soul Healing I warn readers that they are in danger when they take pharmaceuticals. What people don't realize is that these items contain painkillers. At some point people will have to realize that over the counter drugs and prescribed pharmaceuticals are derived from roots and herbs.

Onions became a part of my life after the illness. They have some of the properties of garlic. I especially like purple onions because they not only have more flavor, but they are also more potent. Purple onions have quercetine. That is why they were so popular with the original Indians. Our people were scientists. The Western Indians used it for its quinine content on the skin of the onion. The original Indians were and are still Black. There is a lot of confusion about this. A book needs to be written if it hasn't been already. See the book by Suzar. It is important that this be known because we don't give our ancestors credit where it is due. Indigenous peoples were kind enough to share their knowledge and how are they paid back? Natives rarely benefit from the knowledge they impart, whether it's inventions or medicinal knowledge. I like to take every opportunity to give credit where it is due.

Read Labels

One reason I wrote The Mis-educated Consumer is because I wanted to bring attention to the problem of not reading labels. The general rule is "if you cannot pronounce it" don't consume it. Our forefathers did not have to deal with so many chemicals in food. No study has been done on the impact this bombardment has on our health. It may be years before we discover the true impact of it all.

The greatest healer with the quickest result for me is wheat grass. I chew wheat grass since I don't have a real juicer. But I do spit out the unchewable. Nevertheless I still get the benefits of detoxification. I can feel my stomach getting healthier. The pain goes away. The indigestion is put in check. Wheat grass has a sweet aftertaste, without the ill effects of processed sugar. It makes the urine smell clean. If your urine is clean, your blood is purified. The make-up of urine and blood are so similar. After two years of self-treatment with herbs, colonics, detoxifying clay, massages and saunas, I increased my intake of green foods. It became obvious that some foods had to be eliminated in order to completely heal. It was time to eliminate, commercialized chocolate, coffee, meat and dairy products from the diet. I had to be strong to say no to doughnuts at the office; no to cappuccinos when in good company; no to foods prepared by precious well-meaning relatives and friends; no to social drinking at networking events. Two years of trying to heal while cheating taught me that there are no short cuts when it comes to health. When nature says it's time to pay, it's time to pay. My own words came back to haunt me, 'how many potato chips does it take before your health goes bad? How many sodas? How much fast foods? Who knew? But your body will speak to you. Many of us ignore the warning signals because we think we are invincible or either we are operating in the negative of emotional issues. Eating when depressed or not eating are sure signs of emotional issues. Even when you fast you should put nutrients in your body. By nutrients I mean bee pollen or algae.

Parsley and Cilantro;
two of my favorite words

Parsley and cilantro are next on my favorite greens list. Oriental cilantro has a citrus after-taste, which is good. Latin cilantro or Caribbean cilantro has such a great aroma. It's like receiving medicine and aromatherapy at the same time. I can say the same thing for mangos and avocados. It is literally heaven on Earth. The vitamin content of these foods is incredible. They have vitamin C, A, and a host of other goodies such as calcium and other minerals. Yucca is a great source of calcium. Adamah recommends that you go on a liquid diet at first, in order to let the intestines rest. The problem with me is I was on a liquid diet; it was just the wrong liquid. I was using commercial juice. These juices pass off as juices but they are really sugar water with a small percentage of juice. Does pineapple juice or any juice in its natural state contain corn syrup? No! They even put corn syrup in dried blueberries. Run from processed foods. Make the juice yourself. There are people who are simply not going to try to give up their luxuries and conveniences. To these people I say, "see you at the grave." They should talk to Adamah the nutritional counselor. One session and they'll be convinced to eat sensibly.

After the Exodus, God gave his people manna. It is described in the Bible as having the taste of cilantro. Keep in mind, cilantro is routinely used by Black Latin Americans to season food, be it meat, vegetables or stew. Hebrews or Jivaros, who crossed over the rivers be it the Red Sea or the Atlantic Ocean, never quite forgot their roots. They learned this art from the Egyptians, who learned it from the Central Africans. Don't get me wrong; cilantro grows in many regions, to include India and the Caribbean.

In Ayurvedic medicine, it was used for digestive problems. Cilantro has also been used for urinary problems, despite all its nutritive qualities. The leaves are used for seasoning. Do not overlook the fact that it has calcium, potassium and magnesium. The seed is used to calm the stomach and to prevent infection. Did I mention it is anti-inflammatory? People have kidney conditions for different reasons. But since the symptoms are so similar, go ahead and benefit from my research.

Invest in Superfoods

Algae detoxify. It is also a form of excellent protein. Blue green algae have enzymes, minerals, amino acids, antioxidants, chlorophyll, and the hard to get B-12. It is a super-food. This food alkalinizes your body. The brown algae lower blood pressure - permanently if you are consistent. My advice to people is learn from my mistakes. Be consistent if you want to live. Some people wait until they are too far gone - not realizing they'll have to work thrice as hard to eliminate the years of toxin build up, pus, dead carcasses, parasites, dead embroyos etc. When people say they're not toxic I give them examples of the water they drink, toothpaste they brush with and their amalgams just to name a few. Tap water has fluoride, and lead plus more. Toothpaste has fluoride. Fruits and vegetables are sprayed with herbicides and pesticides, and then they are wrapped in wax. The 'ides" means killing. So you are essentially eating something that is killed due to a chemical designed to kill what's on top of it in order to make it live. This is the same practice of killing the patient while trying to cure or save him with chemotherapy and dialysis.

People who process sugar, salt and flour are essentially removing nutrients, just to turn around and put it back in except in an inferior form that does not cause the proliferation of life.

I am glad I listened to Dr. Sebi's lecture. He teaches that we are electrical beings. Thus, our food should be electric. If something does not resonate an electrical vibe, it should not be consumed. Foods that should fall in line with this but do not are hybrid foods [beets, carrots, garlic]. Electrical foods lose their power if you cook them. I recommend these as transitional foods, because they help heal. Adamah will make you eat only original foods, especially if you are really toxic. You can tell how toxic you are by your ph level. She can show you how you can measure it. Dr Sebi also recommends eating original foods only. As a mother, I tend to allow transitional stages so you can adapt. I'm not sure if this is good or bad. I guess my motherly nature makes me adapt the all-inclusive attitude.

If pristine salt helps a great number of people, then, it might help you. If you are teachable and follow instructions, there is no reason why you shouldn't have the same benefits. There is nothing wrong with sharing information that might benefit others. Think of it this way; neither the shamams nor the curanderas need a doctor's diploma or approval. They did what they were trained to do, or what they visualized as messages from the plant world and so on. They listened to their dreams while passing on long held knowledge. It doesn't matter to me if this book goes out of print, so long as it gets to a significant number of people who need it.

I have received in dreams messages about healing with raspberry, purple lettuce and salt. It took me a long time to even pay attention to these dreams. The dream itself stood out as a revelation. However, it sounded too far-fetched to me that I could cure my organ with purple lettuce and raspberry. Well, I dare you to do a search on its contents and health benefits! They each address the exact symptoms I was having! Kidney malfunction. I was told my organ was no good in a dream before the doctors discovered it! Stubborn me did not heed. That's why later, after I found out what I had been missing, I wrote a poem called "Instincts."

Right now I am in a sharing mood, because I am old and life is short. We can go at any time. Most upright people want to leave a dent in the world and make a difference. Perhaps this is my dent. Speaking of dreams, I once had a revelation of a past life where I was doing presentations in Egypt, using laser beams. There was more but I'll spare you the details. Everyone does not believe in ancient societies, yet the mythical Troy was unearthed. The problem nowadays is that we are stuck in the belief in a two dimensional world. That's the only reason I put together "Soul Healing." Many of us indigo babies are saying the same thing. We seem to be accessing the akhashic records mentally. Hopefully by 2012 most of us would have healed. God knows the world needs healing. Part of that healing is cleansing. What happens above applies below. Our internal bodies need cleansing and so do our minds. We need a spiritual cleansing, not necessarily a religious cleansing. Religion implies rite without meaning, just going through the motions. We have got to get our heads right if we are to survive this turmoil and future upheavals. Every era has challenges. To deal with the stress you can study and learn from the past. Immorality brought down many nations. As we watch the floods, tsunamis, spontaneous fires, and other stressors, we can look up. Vherivea stated that the God instructed Noah to construct the window of the Ark at the top of the Ark. This was a deliberate attempt on God's part to teach Noah that no matter how bad the storms get around us, we must always look up. In Spanish there is a song that says "open your eyes (wake up), look up." I say all this to say part of healing comes from your mindset.

Visualization

The majority of diseases are stemming from the mind. We get scared and toxins are created. We feel anxiety and toxins are created. We get angry and toxins are created. We feel sad and we overeat, which creates toxins. But you can change things around. This brings to mind a poem I wrote called - Change Can Be Good.

The mind can achieve whatever it visualizes. We are co-Creators. We create our own realities. I say this as the opening line to one of my poems Responding To Your Mission and it is true. If we think we will have a bad day we usually do. That's because the mind gets ready for whatever experience you expect. Feed the brain junk and you will feel junkie. It doesn't know the difference. This is why hypnosis is so effective. The brain follows suggestions. Why do you think commercials are so powerful? Why do you think corporations pay millions for short messages during Super Bowl? For the same reason some companies advertise, advertise, advertise. It works. Corporations have learned that people are not people for the most part. They are sheeple. So if we reverse negative thinking, we experience great results. You don't even have to believe it. But the body will follow in action commensurate with whatever we are feeding the mind. One powerful revelation I got was a message that said, "You can alyss blood through the power of the mind." That says it all. Sometimes I think a thought and then I hear a poem about it. Sometimes I think a thought and then someone else writes a poem about it. I saw The Minority Report before it came out. Part of what it says is in one of my poems. I used to think the government was remote viewing my brain because so much that was in my mind was coming out in movies and government reports. I can't tell you every experience I had in this short book but you get the picture. Sometimes I get tired of this cleansing period but it is necessary for progress. If we are trying to be progressive then why do we watch violent movies? If it causes anxiety, then it is not of God. It is that simple. When you watch scary movies, or gory or violent movies or simply people screaming at each other, your body produces a rush of blood to certain vessels in preparedness for flee or fight. Your bodily response does not know the difference between the movie and reality. Toxins are created in your body for a potential life threatening events. The bad news is, the brain does not know the difference. So be careful what you watch or what you let your children watch. Being good is a choice. The company you keep shows the state of mind that you are in.

You Become What You Eat

People who feel like screaming for no apparent reason are probably delivering that which they consumed - death of carcasses. When an animal dies while screaming or in a state of fear, they emit certain toxins. To eat meat nowadays is incomprehensible. In ancient times, animals were not put in a state of fear when killed. The kosher way of killing and preparing meat meant you ingest little toxins compared to now. The blood is drained. Jews and Muslims can tell you that the life is in the blood as the Creator affirmed. Today's animal factories don't care if an animal is diseased. They just cut that part out. Even still, even after going through the kosher procedure, meat is not good for people with kidney problems. If you have a kidney malfunction, you have too much protein in your urine (the blood). How do you think the protein got there? There is no such thing as too much protein from a vegetarian diet. The Maker put vitamins in the plants in proportionate amounts. Something should begin to click. There are people that just weren't meant to be carnivorous, just as some animals weren't meant to be carnivorous. Ever notice how healthy herbivores are? It is not until vegetarians move to big cities that their health suffer. When you think about it, if people really want to be healthy, they could just visit their local farmer's market.

Then there are those who feel like screaming due to stress. Staying stress free should be a goal for anyone who wants to eliminate disease out of his life. As a man thinketh...so is his reality. Life itself began with a thought. If you know negatrons [negative people], get them out of your life. This is a matter of life and death. Ever feel a negative vibe from someone? There's your evidence right there that thoughts are real! Ever been extremely happy just to feel drained as soon as you are around a particular person? Your digestion stops. It works the same way with fear and work situations that are dreadful. Fear and anxiety will paralyze you. I wrote a poem called Fear Is A Sin and another one that begins "We create our own realities." I challenge you to write something inspiring and then read it now and then. Malachi once said the best way to learn something is to teach it.

Music Therapy

Music, art and aromatherapy are just a few ways to de-stress. What you smell can change your mood. What we smell can change our feelings. Mary Magdalene knew the science of aromatherapy well. Bad smells cause depression and bad moods in general. Did you know that brain waves change simply by what the brain smells? Some smells are so powerful; they can stimulate the pineal gland. Christ/Krst received Frankincense. That should tell you something about aromatherapy. The Earth herself provides us with sensuous scents through flowers and resins. We named our store Sensuous Scents and Sights. When I feel anxious I inhale essential oils that heighten my mood, such as citrus smells or musky smells. I like the smell of amber and sandalwood. As a May baby, and being a Taurus, you can just picture me in the garden smelling flowers. In fact, one of my favorite things to do as a child was to go to a nearby garden. Every possible color was in that garden. As you inhale essential oils you are ingesting life's medicines. I tried flower therapy such as consuming flower essence in liquid form. The results surprised me. I thought the lady at the health food store was just trying to make a sale. Flower essences actually changed my mood and how healthy my kidney felt.

Gems And Stones

Using gems and stones to de-stress is also useful. Some people relate to crystals. I am certainly one of them. The crystal came to me to reveal itself. In a like manner, the mineral kingdom may communicate with you. You may have a dream. Do not ignore your dreams. What I am trying to say is that at the right time, the mineral kingdom will come and communicate with you. So will animals, birds and the insect world. People are surprised to hear that I can communicate with mammals, butterflies, eagles, praying mantis and ants.

Visualization has certainly helped me. Even when I was not eating totally correct. My breathing would improve as soon as I thought about eating an orange or wheat grass. I would think, "wait! I haven't even taken a bite yet!" Then I learned how powerful the mind is. I also learned that we attract that which we think about. I recommend "The Secret" to you as given to me in the form of a DVD by Adamah, the nutritional counselor. So yes Lord, I have lived up to my poem that says, "Try nutritional counseling, hydrotherapy...[Health Consciousness]." Want to hear about a few miracles? I have had two angels pass vibrations through me with their minds or hand, and instinctively I healed or felt a surge of serotonin. I myself also healed my daughter of an ugly rash that disappeared instantly when she was little as I waved my hand over her with ash. Whatever your belief system, know that you too can develop your higher god /goddess self. Yeshua/Jesus said we shall perform bigger miracles than him, if we are truly his disciples. People frown on "miracles" or that which they do not understand because they have fallen prey to the conspiracy of Lucifer to blot out anything that is harmonious. He is the father of chaos. Everything negative about you can be balanced out. All knowledge shall come out just before 2012 if it hasn't already. The mischief-makers may protest. But those who have an advantage over others are predictable. God prophesied that this would happen. They try in every way to blotch out anything Godly. In the last days the opposers will sell you anything. They'll pimp you with fake hearts, fake livers and false ideas [The Blind Man and The Pimp]. They'll sell you anything because they know they have very little time left. But soon many will realize that saving the environment is the only alternative. You'll run from genetically engineered foods. These foods have no seeds and no message to convey. Seeds are messengers. They are the Earth Angels. Your body will not operate properly without original foods. Go anywhere but America, eat fruits or vegetables and you'll see what I mean. The aroma is stronger. The energy is more intense. The health benefits multiply. There is something in the seeds and in the soil. Both of these factors have been tampered with in America.

Sun Therapy

The sun comes to mind when it comes to health. I basked in the sunlight more than ever during my illness. In other words, when I wanted to get better I took advantage of sunlight. Think about it, sunlight gets rid of mold! Nothing else gets rid of mold. The sun doesn't shine in corners of houses. That's why in Biblical times prophets were instructed to tear down a house where mold has crept. The sun is powerful. Our ancestors knew the science of the sun. I noticed overseas where it is sunny; I ate less and had more energy while staying out in the sun. After a while, I noticed my energy was coming from the sun. I felt worst away from the sun and vice versa. The sun gives you vitamin D. Vitamin D is crucial to kidney sufferers. If this is not you, have you considered that you might be anti-life? Think about it, plants grow under the sun. Need I say more?

Avoid Negative People

The complainers do not want a solution. They only want to present problems. They are toxic to you. Your paying attention to them will be your downfall. The best thing to do is get away from them if you want to heal. Bless the Lord who purifies the Earth and cares for his servants.

Stay Clean

After you cleanse yourself and replace your eating habits with sensible ones, show gratitude for health by not dumping into your body any more. Do not put chocolate bars into your system. The idea is to get out alive. If you must die why not die of a natural death as opposed to dying in agony. Trust me, you'll regret your actions once that pain sets in. The cramping will be unbearable along with everything else. If you no longer put junk in your body, your body will thank you by breathing right and free of obstruction. Digesting foods at all kinds of hours all day or at the wrong time makes your body works harder. It is never at rest and thus you suffer physically. At some point you will have to give your body a rest. For this reason, Adamah recommends that you go on a liquid diet for a while.

Elijah Muhammad and many others have emphasized giving your digestive track a break. Elijah wrote that you should eat one meal a day. When your body finally gives out in agony because you overworked the intestines, you will think about these activities you engaged in. Life and death has everything to do with your guts. Food can be used as a medicine or as poison depending on what you use. Processed foods are not original foods. Feed a dog processed food and see how long he lives. Feed a cat processed foods and watch him throw up. All animals go to the yard when they're sick - to eat something green. Green foods have chlorophyll in them. Chlorophyll is the equivalent of blood in the plant kingdom. Yes, the life is in the blood. You know if a plant is sick or not. If it is sick you don't eat it. Some people lay fallow, doing nothing because supposedly fate is ordained. They're not seeing the bigger picture. You were given free will. That right there should tell you something. How you chose to act or not act will determine whether you are accomplishing your mission. My destiny card tells me I will deal with issues of health and creativity. It's either I stay sick or help people get well, or I hide my talents or showcase my creativity by writing, drawing etc. In other words, if you don't use your talents to help humanity, no one will know what your talents are, or that you ever existed. What's worst, you won't help the world; and you'll die a failure. I hope you have benefited in some way. I hope I have prolonged your life long enough for you to accomplish your mission. Remember, time is running out. The Golden Age is approaching. The Age of Aquarius is at hand. Will you be of the ones who bend time for higher purposes or to cause confusion? The Akhashic record is replete with examples of people who thought nobody was watching. Whether you believe in karma, reincarnation, God, Christ, the Devil, Buddha, Krishna, science, magic or whatever the only truth is "everything is everything," as Michael Baisden and Malachi like to say. After winter must come spring says the lady with the heavy message, Lauren Hill. We believe in cycles. Eventually you'll come around [pun intended]. Face it, we are born. We live. We die. You eat poison you will die. It is that simple.

The Price of Reverting

Don't revert back to milk. Milk was made for babies. Baby cows and baby goats are not us. Just when I thought everything was peachy, I find myself squealing in agony, after drinking milk. The pain was in my lower back. The fear I had was that my kidney was infected. By this time, I knew where my kidneys were located. The pain was in the kidney. I recall what my urologist had said. "Bring yourself to the hospital when your kidney gets infected." It is not infected yet." "You will know." The voice kept echoing, as I struggled to move around, back and forth to work. These were the most painful days of my life, next to having a baby. Actually, I don't know which was worst. "On a scale of one to ten, how much does it hurt?" asked the nurse. "Eleven," I shouted. Keep in mind that I am a naturalist. I do not smoke, drink etc. Before I took myself to ER, I had used a lot of oregano oil and garlic as antibiotics. And trust me, it eased the pain. Whatever, was going on prior to that, I am sure that the oregano oil and the garlic killed it along with the olive leaf and Echinacea. What kills me is how doctors always take the credit. Or they have the nerve to ask you "what did you use?" I believe this is how they have learned so much over the years. They study us Black Indians like crazy, just as the Orientals do. Everyone knows we are one big experiment. Then they write books and take all the credit. So okay, I can write a book too, based on my ancestral knowledge. Why should the doctors get all the credit? They use our symbols, the snake over the staff. It stands for the kundalini. Some of you look at voodoo and cringe. That's because you have been brainwashed into thinking that any black science is bad. They trick you with word association to make everything black bad. Black magic; the art of the Blacks. What you don't know is that there is a worldwide conspiracy to keep Blacks oppressed. Our knowledge has been suppressed. The time is here for the truth to come out. I am Mother Earth. So is Adamah, so is Queen Afua and so on and so on. We are each playing a role of some sort of archetype found in our hidden sciences. We each came here under contract. Those who get sick do so because they have fallen asleep or are under a spell. As you wake up, as you see certain symbols, the keys begin to unlock. It is okay to acknowledge your true God and Goddess selves. Take hold of your staff, become the royal co-creator and co-creatrix and never let go. Give up the bad diets. You are no longer in chain. The chains that bind are breaking. We are experiencing, the mental freedom. Let us act like the hue-man beings that we are.

I not only took oregano oil and tea internally, along with garlic; but I also applied it externally to the kidney area and lower back to the left side where it hurt. You will not believe the relief experienced. Just know that you have to be consistent with it. And do not be afraid to take a larger dose than prescribed; as natural remedies have no side effects. Always consult a professional if not sure. For those who cannot afford an alternative doctor just know that people have treated conditions with herbs for eons before modern technology or modern medicine. Alternative doctors are worth every penny. It's your life we are talking about. Don't you love yourself? Do you want the best for yourself? Think of what's in your best interest. People are finally taking their lives back. When you buy cranberry juice, buy it undiluted from the health food store. It is not sweet, but it works. If you have a sweet tooth, use honey. But always dilute it with water. The amount of water depends on the intensity of your condition. I have also found that slippery elm inserted in the vagina is helpful with burning sensations. Marshmallow root is also good to take internally for urinary track infections. Some women are closely built, so any food with e.coli will attack the bladder. Doesn't this make you want to quit eating meat altogether? It may sound silly to repeat the known, but females should wipe from front to back, using water always like the Muslims use estinga. You can always spray yourself with a bottle of water. It also doesn't hurt to sit in water.

Oregano, Garlic & Lemon to the Rescue

During this painful episode I realized I would need something stronger than what I had been taking. It was not a kidney infection as according to the Emergency Room doctor. A urinary tract infection was in full swing. She seemed upset that I had been treating myself naturally. "But at least I kept it in check," I retorted. She couldn't deny it. Most people's kidneys would have been gone by now. This is two years after the five percent function. So I put a bunch of garlic and strong oregano oil into my enema. The following day I did the same thing. Later, I started alternating the oregano enema with the clay. I did this three times a week, while drinking oregano tea with garlic. I ate nothing. My vitamins came from natural supplements. It was liquid diet or die. The supplements included bee pollen, green powders such as alfalfa and barley grass. Yes, I gave myself a blood transfusion using barley grass. What this means is that barley grass has the same effect as getting a blood transfusion. But that wasn't enough. What finally killed it was the oregano oil, garlic and concentrated cranberry juice. The one that had the strongest effect was the garlic eaten raw. It is strong so I had to drink tea behind it. I used no white sugar to sweeten the tea. Honey directly from the comb became my best friend. Sometimes I would use dates to sweeten it. Later, I began to eat the dates and figs. By this time I was aware that dates and figs fix stomach problems. At the emergency room I had discovered that my kidney problems stem from a blockage in my stomach that is preventing the kidney from functioning properly. They think I was born with it. Tests remain to be taken. My point is I didn't have to go into dialysis to repair my kidney. This is 2007. The kidney function of five percent occurred in 2005.

How to Cure a Serious Bladder Attack

One thing is for sure. When all is said and done, and nothing else works, here is what you do. Stop eating. Take nothing but oregano tea, oregano oil (diluted!), garlic and lemon, one at a time or intermittently. If you fear you will starve, take bee pollen and or Irish moss with bladder wrack. That's it. The fear of starvation is unfounded. This irrational fear is driving us to our death. Cooked foods take us to our graves. Ironically, the less you eat the longer you live.

Feast or famine is a concept from the Ice Age period. In reality, there is more abundance than lack. Unfortunately a few control the world resources – roughly four percent of the people. They create lack, and waste land by grazing animals. Thus forcing us to take pus in our veins as vaccinations. No one likes this system. But they remain quiet.

Conclusion

I think it is impressive that I did not succumb to dialysis whereas others did at 20 and 10 percent function. If I die of stomach cancer, then at least I can say I avoided the machine that takes you quicker to your grave. While in the Emergency Room at the hospital, I thought it was all over. I was supposed to follow up right away with a specialist. I did not for lack of money, among other things. That proved to be a blessing in disguise. This is because I winded up self-treating. I certainly appreciated the painkillers, the saline solution, which is really food grade hydrogen peroxide, and the antibiotics. But the pain persisted until I took the oregano oil and garlic. The concentrated cranberry was merely the icing on the cake. Do you know I have been drinking cranberry juice forever? That is why I say, it was a combination of all the above. Even before I went to the Emergency Room, I noticed that the oregano oil and garlic were ameliorating the condition. Oregano has been proven to be an antibiotic. As a matter of fact, it was proven to work where other antibiotics fail. I warned the nurse that I had been taking natural antibiotics, so she won't try to take all the credit for my improvement. But I always notice how they become extremely interested in natural cures. This is how they develop their medicines. She is not the only one interested. Doctors show a great deal of interest, too. Eventually I did confess that I used Echinacea as well. But I never revealed the use of oregano. They need to pay me for all this information just like I am paying them for their service. We Black people are poor because we give away too much information. So much so, until people take us for granted. And we don't know how to become consultants. But other groups will do it in a heartbeat. I find myself giving away priceless information at people's beckoning. I love helping people. Well, now you can read about the wonders of oregano, something I grew up with. People are charging top dollars for it, because they know its value. I am telling you that you can go in Mexican stores and it get for two dollars or less. I have given you valuable advice. I have told you what real salt looks like and how you never have to fear overdosing off of it. This is the stuff people paid gold for. We are made of 70 percent water. Salt is condensed seawater, which has healing capacity. You now know that kidneys need water to function properly. You now know not to ever eat white sugar, stay away from meat and dairy. You will lose weight for the first time in a long time. You will buy organic and eat raw vegetables and fruits. You will obtain these from the international stores. You now know that some fruits are cheaper at the health food stores. And you know that you can find organics vegetation at health food stores as well as international stores. You know that herbs are more potent at international stores since they grow in mineral rich soil. You are also aware that they don't genetically manipulate foods as Americans do. Unfortunately for Americans people do not want their foods nor their lifestyle of obesity obsessive eating which leads dis-ease. You now know that fat does not mean healthy. Hopefully you see the value in not being carnivorous. You were made aware that meat takes four hours to digest. You learned how unnatural it is for hue-mans to be carnivorous. Armed with the knowledge of how to lose weight and how exercise gives you energy, you should be on your way to a fun, healthy lifestyle. Much love to you, peace and success. May the Aquarian Age bring you life giving minerals like it did me. God himself was bathing me in minerals, who said, "This is my daughter, in whom I am very pleased." We are all godchildren. Everyone was destined to be great. The question is will they lean toward the wrong side of the equation in greatness, will they be mediocre, leaving no trace of ever being on the earth, or will they live to be their true god selves. Telling a person to be humble and not achieve is like telling a flower not to bloom. It is cheating nature. It is cheating others from the beauty they could be enjoying. So go ahead and bloom. I am taking my place. I am blooming...just as I was ordered to. The world is my stage. This is my destiny. In the room are shades. And I am the container.

When my doctor first told me my kidney would have to be removed if it got infected, that was in 2005. Since then I have been using alternative modalities. I did ask a lot of questions. He finally admitted that some people fight it while others don't do so well. What I did not know is that simply eliminating dairy foods and meat would make such a difference. Years of indoctrination have to be reversed. Many people have become vegans, but many more still have to wake up. The reality we need to wake up to is that being carnivorous is unnatural. Once I left meat and dairy products alone and white flour, I began to lose weight for the first time. I was weighing 136, which is a lot for my height of 5'1. When I saw 125 on the scale, I was elated. It meant I could finally fit my clothes! At first I cheated, while on the Adamah program. But then I found I was only cheating myself so...it was a matter of checking out totally or checking out her program for what it was worth. It wasn't easy for me because of the years of negative indoctrination. You see I had been totally brainwashed over and over again. It starts with low self-esteem. I was told I was the ugliest thing that ever lived on earth. After years of hearing this something sunk in, even though I didn't believe it at first.

You can empower yourself by choosing what you will ingest. You have been shown unconventional alternatives. Unconventional does not mean bad. It means options. You also have the option of not watching TV so you won't be brainwashed.

You too, can experience health - a feeling of well being. We have felt so bad for so long that we have forgotten what health feels like. Some people are so polluted inside that they eat junk as soon as they feel better. This is called balancing the junk equation or rather - an addiction. You are literally addicted to feeling bad. The good Lord said once you are healed "go and sin no more."

I am thankful that I was able to turn my life around, while inspiring you. We, the original Indians who are and always have been Black, have always practiced a good, well-rounded diet. I hope you came out of this knowing that beans are not the only protein substitute. Vegetables, seeds and bee pollen all have plenty of proteins. That statement was for those who were led to believe that they can not live without protein. As a matter of fact, you should re-think the pyramid of food lies, because it has led you down the wrong path of a carnivorous lifestyle. Like other groups who come to America, we too, suffer health ills. Africans of Nigeria are healthier than Afro-Americans. This goes to show that diet is one of the components that keep people healthy. We, the West Indians/Caribbean Islanders, Latin Americans have a great diet, but are not immune to the ill effects of an American diet. All other groups, not only eat better than Americans, but they also move around more. So, unless Americans change their sedentary lifestyle and their love for eating animal flesh and by-products, they will continue to suffer from kidney disease and other conditions. Kidney disease is a silent killer. You may have it and not know it. Follow what your alternative doctor tells you. Eat raw and your life should improve, especially if you detoxify yourself. Consult an alternative doctor regarding the PH balance equation.

Bibliography

Africa, Llaila <u>African Holistic Health.</u> Maryland Sea Island
    Information Group - Adesegun, Johnson & Koram
    Publishers, 1983

Castleman, Michael <u>Las Hierbas Que Curan [Healing Herbs].</u>
    Pennsylvania Rodale Press, 1991

Dixon, Barbara M. L.D.N., R.D. <u>Good Health For African
    Americans.</u> New York Crown Publishers, Inc. 1994

Guttlieb, Bill New <u>Choices in Natural Healing.</u> Pennsylvania
    Rodale Press, 1995

Hausman, Patricia <u>Healing Foods: The Ultimate Authority O The
    Curative Power Of Nutrition.</u> Pennsylvania
    A Dell Book – division of Bantan Doubleday, 1989

Kennedy, Robert Jr. "Autism, Mercury, and Politics The Boston
    Globe Boston http://www.boston.com/news/globe/editorial
    opinion/ped/articles/2005/07/01/autism me rcury_and
    politics?mode=PF 2005

    http://www.themeatrix1.com

Muhammad, Elijah <u>Message To The Blackman In America.</u>
    Maryland Secretarius MEMPS Publications, 1965

Muhammad, Elijah <u>How To Eat To Live.</u> Chicago Muhammad
    Temple Of Islam No. 2, 1992

Prevention Health Libraries <u>Home Remedies.</u> Pennsylvania Rodale
    Press Inc, 1998

Robinson, Helen/Queen Afua <u>Sacred Woman: A Guide to Healing
    The Femenine Body And Spirit</u> New York:
    One World - The Ballantine Publishing Group, 2000

Simone, Charles B., MD <u>Cancer and Nutrition</u> New York
 Avery Publishing Group, 1992

Trivieri, Larry Jr., John W. Anderson <u>Alternative Medicine</u>
 Berkley-Pennsylvania Rodale PressInc – Prevention Health
 Libraries, 1998

Truddeau, Kevin <u>Natural Cures "They Don't Want You To Know
 About"</u>. Illinois: Aliance Publishing Group, 2004

Young, Robert <u>The PH Miracle.</u> New York
 Warner Wellness – Time Warner Book Group, 2002

Recommended Readings

Heal Thyself For Health and Longevity,
Queen Afua

What Your Doctor May Not Tell
You About Hypertension,
Mark Houston, MD

Natural Health Remedies
Janet Maccaro Phd CVC

The Natural Pharmacy
Alan Gaby, MD

http://www.themeatrix1.com

The PH Factor

Index

engineered, 53
. Fluoride, 42
acid, 20
alcohol, 27
algaes, 87
aluminum, 40
amalgams, 41
amino acids, 133
anaerobic bacteria, 36
anti-biotic properties, 121
anti-inflammatory, 134
anti-microbial, 61
aspirin, 90
autism, 47. *See* vaccination
BEE POLLEN, 119
bladder, 145
blood pressure, 5, 6, 16, 21, 22, 23, 43, 61, 63, 67, 81, 86, 94, 96, 97, 115, 118, 125, 129, 131, 141, 142, 144, 148, 149, 151, 152, 157
blood toxicity, 133
bucchu, 149
calcium, 113
capillaries, 21
Cascara Sagrada, 98
castor oil, 98
cellular toxicity, 133
Charcoal, 127
chelating, 87

chemical, 23, 34, 35, 45, 49, 74, 83, 94, 115, 127, 129, 136, 148, 149, 157
chlorine, 23
chlorophyll, 138
chocolate, 108
cholesterol., 140
Cigarette, 27
cilantro, 156
circulation, 83
CKLS, 94
clay, 81, 103
Cloves, 80
coconut, 107
Co-Enzyme Q10, 131
Coffee, 52
colonic, 132
Constipation, 30
contaminants, 91
Conventional medicine, 8, 61
Dandelion, 97
dialysis, 5, 9, 12, 18, 27, 47, 60, 62, 63, 64, 67, 68, 73, 79, 85, 101, 117, 138, 140, 143, 158, 169, 170
digest, 18
digestive system. *See* digest
diuretics, 85
DNA, 44
drugs, 137
e.coli, 30

edema, 6, 65, 97, 122, 146, 149, 150
electromagnetic waves, 25
enzymes, 115
fermentation., 144
fiber, 54, 106
filtering, 84
free radicals, 125
fulvic acid, 137
Garlic, 144
Germanium, 145
glutathione, 133
glycerin, 76
heavy metal, 87
HEAVY METALS, 24
Himalayan salt, 23
horsetail, 97
Hydrogen Peroxide, 93
hydrotherapy, 132
immunizations, 70
intestinal toxification, 133
Kidney disease, 173
stones, 173
kidney meridian, 112. *See* kidney disease
magnesium, 106
manganese, 106
meat, 29
micro waved food, 39
micronutrients, 68
milk, 36
mineral, 119
mold!, 163
MSM, 146
mustard seed, 137
Natural antibiotic, 43
neutraceudicals, 48
nutrient absorption, 35
Olive leaf, 22

oregano, 80
organ meats, 126. *See* purine
over-eat, 24
oxalates, 12, 105, 127
oxygen, 38
PAD, 124. *See* kidney meridian
paint thinner, 71
parasites,, 55
ph balance, 137
phytochemical, 68
potassium, 120
processed foods, 40
protein, 29
pumpkin seed, 117
purifying, 85
purine., 126
purple lettuce, 130
quercetine, 126
radiation, 135
raspberries, 130
Real salt, 90
sauna, 146
scavenger, 37
Selenium, 136
sorrel, 100
STRESS, 20
sugar, 28, 110
table salt, 74
Tobacco, 49. *See* cigarette
toxic, 7, 11, 18, 33, 37, 38, 40, 41, 48, 67, 73, 80, 81, 84, 94, 98, 112, 116, 118, 123, 127, 128, 130, 133, 135, 157, 158, 165
urine, 19
vaccinations, 41
vitamin D, 69, 163
vitamin P, 120

water, 6, 7, 9, 10, 11, 21, 23,
    24, 31, 36, 40, 41, 42, 45, 48,
    55, 66, 68, 70, 71, 76, 82, 83, 84,
    88, 91, 94, 95, 96, 97, 98, 103,
    114, 116, 122, 123, 127, 129,
    131, 132, 133, 134, 137, 142, 146,
    147, 148, 149, 150, 151, 156, 157,
    168, 171
Wormwood, 107
X-rays, 21

About the Author

Mercedes M. Hawkins was born Mercedes Maria Beato-Frias in Santo Domingo, Dominican Republic, otherwise known as Kiskeya. The sixth child of seven, graduated from Georgetown University with a degree in Sociology.

From the beginning Mercedes expressed a liking for the arts. This includes writing, painting, drawing, sculpting, dancing, songwriting, and performing spoken word. She is the author of Divine Spoken Word. Other credits include Editor-in-Chief Spectrum aka Corral, Organic Times newsletter editor and other writings.

Her song Times Are Trying won a local mention at The Cotton Club. You may have seen her perform at Yin Yang, A-Hop, funerals, retirements, graduations or at Black History month's Paul Robeson auditorium at the Arts Exchange in Atlanta, Georgia.

HOW I AVOIDED DIALYSIS: And You Can Too
    Mercedes Hawkins

Available at;

> **Life's Essentials** health food store
> 2329 Cascade Rd., SW Atlanta,
> Ga, Telephone (404)753-2269
> http://www.youtube.com/user/sacredgeometryqueen?feature=
> mhee

Here is an order form for Mercedes's publications

Order Form

Title	Price	Qty
HOW I AVOIDED DIALYSIS : And you can too	$24.51..	_
Divine Spoken Word	$10.00..	_
Jena 6: A Sign Of The Times	$5.00..	_
Biography Of A Warrior	$12.00..	_
Calendar	$15.00..	_
Single poems	$2.00..	_